MW01195199

Padre Pio and I
Memoirs of a Spiritual Son

The information in this book is based on experiences of the author.

Published by: Adolfo Affatato
Website: www.PadrePioAndI.org

Formatting: Brand Bionic, LLC | www.brandbionic.com

Additional contact information in the back of the book.

Padre Pio and I

MEMOIRS OF A SPIRITUAL SON

Adolfo Affatato

www.PadrePioAndI.org

To my wife, Franca,
To my children, Francesco Pio
and Maria Grazia Pia,
To Lucia and to my beloved granddaughters
Francesca and Beatrice

And, finally, thanks to my dear Eda
with paternal affection

Franca Affatato

Timeline of Saint Pio of Pietrelcina

May 25, 1887: Maria Giuseppa Di Nunzio, wife of Grazio Forgione, gives birth to a son in town of Pietrelcina, near Benevento in the region of Campania in southern Italy.

May 26, 1887: The child is baptized in the church of Sant'Anna in Pietrelcina with the name, Francesco, after St. Francis of Assisi.

January 6, 1903: Francesco enters the novitiate in the Franciscan Capuchin Order in Morcone.

January 22, 1903: Investiture: Francesco dons the habit and receives his religious name, Brother Pio.

January 27, 1907: Pio makes his solemn profession (final vows) in the Capuchin Order.

August 10, 1910: He is ordained a priest in the cathedral of Benevento.

August 14, 1910: Padre Pio celebrates his first Mass in church of Our Lady of the Angels in Pietrelcina.

1910-1915: Padre Pio remains home in Pietrelcina to recover from mysterious health maladies.

September 20, 1910: He receives the invisible stigmata at the family property in Piana Romana just outside of Pietrelcina; the wounds were painful and would come and go.

November 6, 1915: Padre Pio is called to mandatory military service in the Italian army. Due to poor health, he is eventually declared unfit for military service and is discharged.

February 17, 1916: Padre Pio is assigned to the friary of Sant'Anna in Foggia.

September 4, 1916: He arrives for the first time in "Our Lady of Grace" friary in San Giovanni Rotondo and immediately knows he will remain there for the rest of his life.

August 5, 1918: Padre Pio's heart is pierced by a celestial being holding a steel sword -- a spiritual phenomenon known as "transverberation."

September 20, 1918: While praying before a crucifix in the choir stall overlooking the main altar in the church of "Our Lady of Grace," Padre Pio receives the visible stigmata -- the wounds of Christ on his hands, feet, and side. He is the first priest in the history of the Church ever to receive the stigmata.

1919: News of the stigmata and of Padre Pio's charismatic gifts spreads throughout Italy, and thousands of people begin making their way to the small town.

May 15, 1919: Padre Pio's superiors request medical examinations of his stigmata. He is examined by four doctors during the course of the year.

1923 - 1933: Padre Pio is the victim of calumny and persecution from within the order and the Church.

June 9, 1931: The Holy See prohibits Padre Pio from all activities -- including hearing confessions and having contact with his spiritual children -- except for Mass, which he can only celebrate in private.

July 16 1933: Pope Pius XI reverses the ban, saying, "I have not been badly disposed toward Padre Pio, but I have been badly informed."

January 9, 1940: Work is begun on a new hospital in San Giovanni Rotondo which Padre Pio names, "The Home for the Relief of Suffering." Padre Pio refers to it as his "Grand Earthly Undertaking."

1947: Padre Pio Prayer Groups begin.

May 5, 1956: The hospital is inaugurated and officially opened.

April 23, 1966: Last wedding performed by Padre Pio was the marriage of Adolfo and Franca Affatato in San Giovanni Rotondo.

July 31, 1968: Padre Pio Prayer Groups receive official recognition by the Holy See.

September, 22 1968: Padre Pio celebrates Mass for the last time.

Sept. 23, 1968: At 2:30 am, at the age of eighty-one, Padre Pio dies in his cell in the friary of San Giovanni Rotondo. The guardian states that all traces of the stigmata on Padre Pio's hands, feet and side disappear shortly after his death.

September 26, 1968: Over one hundred thousand people attend Padre Pio's funeral in San Giovanni Rotondo.

March 20, 1983: The official inquiry into the cause of Padre Pio's canonization is opened.

May 23, 1987: Pope John Paul II makes a pilgrimage to San Giovanni Rotondo and prays at Padre Pio's tomb.

April 1997: Padre Pio is declared Venerable.

Dec. 21, 1998: The Congregation for the Cause of Saints approves the scientifically inexplicable healing of Mrs. Consiglia De Martino of Salerno, Italy which serves for Padre Pio's beatification.

May 2, 1999: Padre Pio is beatified by Pope John Paul II.

Dec. 18, 2000: The Congregation for the Cause of Saints approves the healing of seven-year-old Matteo Collela of San Giovanni Rotondo which serves for Padre Pio's canonization.

June 16, 2002: Padre Pio is canonized by Pope John Paul II in St. Peter's before a crowd of 500,000 people.

July 1, 2004: The large modern church -- designed by world-renowned architect, Renzo Piano -- is consecrated in San Giovanni Rotondo.

April 24, 2008: The tomb of Padre Pio is opened up and the body of Padre Pio on display in the crypt in the old church in San Giovanni Rotondo.

April, 2010: Padre Pio's remains are moved to the crypt in the new church in San Giovanni Rotondo where they remain today.

February 8-14, 2016: The remains of Saint Pio are moved outside of San Giovanni Rotondo for the first time ever. They are brought to St. Peter's in Rome for veneration of the faithful for the Extraordinary Jubilee Year of Mercy.

"Then I was crowned by my God,
and my crown was living....
I received the face
and likeness of a new person...
And the thought of truth led me,
and I went after it and wandered not.
And all who saw me were amazed,
and I seemed to them like a stranger.
And He who knew and exalted me,
is the Most High in all His perfection.
And He glorified me by His kindness,
and raised my understanding to the height of truth.
And from there He gave me the way of His steps,
and I opened the doors which were closed.
And I shattered the bars of iron,
for my own shackles had grown hot and melted before me.
And nothing appeared closed to me,
because I was the opening of everything.*

17th Ode of Solomon

Contents

Foreword

A spiritual encounter on a train to Rome

For the first time, "Padre Pio and I" is now available in English.

Padre Pio comes alive in these pages through the eyes of a close acquaintance, spiritual child Adolfo Affatato. These stories go behind the scenes to get an inside look into the personal life of the great saint Padre Pio as few had people had known him.

This book was originally published in Italian. Our story is how two Americans -- on a train -- were asked to print this book in English, to share these intimate stories about Padre Pio.

God works in amazing ways. Such was the case the day we met Adolfo and his wife, Franca, on a train to Rome in September of 2013.

They were on their way to Rome to present his book about Saint Padre Pio to a Cardinal who would give it to Pope Francis. We had just completed our first visit to the Padre Pio Shrine in San Giovanni Rotondo and were traveling to Rome also.

What happened over the next three-hour train ride could not have been scripted. The time on the train with Adolfo was surreal. We learned about his very personal 15-year relationship with Padre Pio. He showed us his first class relics of Padre Pio. The last wedding ever performed by Padre Pio was Adolfo's wedding. Pope John Paul II asked Adolfo to spend some private time with him sharing Adolfo's stories about Padre Pio. Adolfo knew Padre Pio well...very well.

We were blessed and amazed to be in the company of someone who knew Padre Pio as well as Adolfo did. As a result of this "chance" meeting, his book is now available in America and for other English-speaking readers.

First, let us explain why we were on that train. We had traveled from America to Italy for a personal holy pilgrimage that we arranged ourselves. We were seeking intercessions of the saints through prayer for a very difficult family situation.

Our daughter was in her mid-30's and married. She had a master's degree, and had been a teacher for 15 years. She was never a problem. Her life changed and became convoluted. Out of respect for her we will detail no more. She estranged herself from us from us for several years and we lost all contact with her. It was a very difficult time for us.

We were very concerned for her well-being. We did almost everything we could to intervene. Finally we turned it over to God. Carrying this cross was only possible with prayer, our family and friends, and holy people we met along the way. God does hold you up at your darkest times of life.

1

We decided for our European trip to list all the saints we loved and were the dearest to our hearts. Number one was St. Padre Pio. We traveled to San Giovanni Rotondo and spent time in prayer. We visited his tomb. We prayed in the old church. We prayed to the crucifix that Padre Pio prayed to when receiving his stigmata. We were even at the celebration of the 95th anniversary of his stigmata...a true blessing in itself.

After leaving San Giovanni Rotondo, we randomly met Adolfo and his wife at the train station i n Foggia. We asked him for help in getting to the right train to Rome. He showed us the way as they were going to be on the same train. Adolfo sat across the aisle from us. When we saw his Padre Pio book, we attempted a conversation, but we did not speak Italian and he spoke very little English. Eventually, a

Steve and Lynne Pfaff in San Giovanni Rotondo in front of Padre Pio's confessional (Old Santa Maria delle Grazie church).

young man on the train named Luca became our translator between Italian and English with Adolfo.

Our conversation with Adolfo was non-stop. It was as if time had stopped and we were the only ones on the train. The stories he shared of Padre Pio and his life with him were amazing. It was as if we were living with Padre Pio ourselves at that very moment.

Before we reached Rome, Adolfo asked if we would like to put his book in English for Americans so more could read his personal stories about this great saint. After departing from this encounter we both said we couldn't tell anyone about this request because they wouldn't believe it anyway. We knew nothing about publishing books. Eventually we were able to unfold this grace and make it a reality. The English edition is now available in America, Italy and other parts of the world.

We later asked him why he asked us to publish the book in America. He said sometimes his heart beats fast as a sign from Padre Pio and he also said," Padre Pio speaks to me". He said he felt that way when we were on the train with him that day. We felt honored and blessed to participate in this project.

2

While on the train to Rome, we told Adolfo our reason for being in Italy and the story of our daughter. We gave him a small picture of her. He said he would pray for her, and would pray to Padre Pio for her. He continued to pray for her since that encounter in September 2013.

When we came back the next year to visit Adolfo in San Giovanni Rotondo, while at the tomb of Padre Pio, Adolfo pulled her picture we gave him the year before out of his wallet and prayed with us at the tomb. While there, one priest told us to be like the "Prodigal Father" upon our reuniting with our daughter. Unknown to us at that time, miracles were already beginning to take shape for us with our daughter.

In the year that followed, the door opened and she said she wanted to see us. With peace, joy and love we are moving forward in our relationship with her and celebrating this reunion. Her life is better and the biggest blessing is she had a baby boy, making us grandparents! This whole turn of events was a miracle for us. We believe through the prayers of many people and especially the intercession of Adolfo and Padre Pio, our story is one of good news.

We are humbly grateful. Our holy pilgrimage has given us many spiritual blessings. We now talk with our daughter almost daily and visit them on a regular basis, even though they live in another state.

Never underestimate the powers of this great saint through his intercession to the Blessed Mother and Jesus Christ. When you read the stories from Adolfo, you will know the saint as few had known him. You will relive intimate moments in Padre Pio's life through the experiences of this spiritual child. For the first time we share Adolfo's true-life stories with English readers all over the world. Read them. Learn from them. Enjoy them.

Miracles happen...we know.

As Padre Pio said: *"My Children, I am close to you. Closer than you can imagine. I am in contact with your mind and am directing your thoughts. I am close to your heart and am counting your heartbeats, so that with all in unison they might lift up a hymn of glory to God the Father Almighty."*

Steve and Lynne Pfaff
Clearwater, FL USA

Acknowledgements

We are blessed to be part of this project of printing this book in English for the first time so even more people can read and hear about Saint Padre Pio through Adolfo's 15 years with him. We want to thank Adolfo and his wife Franca for letting us play a part. We would like to thank Luca de Masi, who translated for us on the train to Rome that day. Without translating Adolfo's conversation, we would not have moved forward.

We would also like to give mention to the person who introduced us to St. Padre Pio over 15 years ago. Her name is Debbie Rosewell a long time friend for over 35 years.

A special thank you goes out to our print translator, Bret Thoman, for his tireless effort. His dedicated work and personal conversations directly with Adolfo in translating the entire book from Italian to English made this book a reality. You can read more about Bret in the back of the book.

We would also like to thank the friary at San Giovanni Rotondo and Padre Paolo Cuvino for their endorsement of this book in English and their desire to have this book available for its visitors in Italy.

We have deep-faith family and friends who have prayed for us and with us. We have been led to some amazing special priests and a nun in Rome, Sr. Gracy, who is a dear friend and so special. So much love and healing has transpired. God is Good! We hope you enjoy this English edition.

Adolfo Affatato with superior Fr. Paolo Cuvino, and Lynne and Steve Pfaff at the Friary in San Giovanni Rotondo during a meeting about translating Adolfo's book into English.

Translator's Introduction

The English edition of Adolfo Affatato's book, *Padre Pio and I*, began after I received a call from Steve Pfaff who said he had recently been to Italy with his wife where he met a gentleman on a train who had known Padre Pio personally. He said that this man, Adolfo Affatato, had been a spiritual son of Padre Pio and had written a book about him in Italian. Steve said that he and his wife were considering having it translated into English, adding, "This is a story that everyone needs to know." He asked me if I would be willing to read it and possibly translate it. As a Secular Franciscan with a strong devotion to Padre Pio, I told Steve I would be delighted to take a look.

As soon as I read the first few chapters, I immediately sensed that this was no ordinary book about Padre Pio. It was not written by a biographer, journalist, or theologian; instead, it was obvious that this was a special book written by a special person who loved Padre Pio personally and deeply. The figure of Padre Pio that emerged was paternal, intimate, and tender.

Although I specialize in translating books on spirituality and the saints, my experience with this one has been different. Any time you translate a book, you have to try to get to know the author -- to get inside their head and understand how they think. And during this process, I had several occasions to meet with Adolfo Affatato to learn how he reasons and how he lives his life. And doing so has enriched my life tremendously.

I felt a kinship with Adolfo the first time we spoke. He comes from the city of Foggia -- some 40 km (25 miles) from San Giovanni Rotondo -- in the region of Apulia (Puglia in Italian). This is the same southern Italian region where my wife, Katia, is from. When I spoke to him, I felt like I was talking to any of my wife's uncles.

Apulia is a long narrow strip of land comprising the ankle of the Italian boot. It is a wonderful land that boasts of ancient history, breathtaking landscapes and seascapes, outstanding food, and numerous saints. Any small town or city alike has some remnant of antiquity: the Greeks, Romans, Saracens and Normans all fought over Apulia for its strategic military position thrust into the western part of the Mediterranean Sea. (Even today there are still a handful of important NATO bases here.) Its confines with the Adriatic Sea to the east and the Ionian Sea to the south make Apulia a great place for seafood as well as an international tourist destination for beach lovers. Its fertile soil and sea ports have led to a rich culinary tradition, and Apulia is a place where its mid-day lunches are as long as the lazy siestas that follow. Pasta like cavatelli and orecchiette with rapini, rich olive oils, cheeses like scamorza and cacciocavallo, wines like Negroamaro, Primitivo and Bombino Nero, and desserts like cartellate, mostaccioli and taralli are all synonymous with Apulia.

Despite the inroads of modernism and secularization, southern Italian culture is still thoroughly Catholic. For pilgrims, there are plenty of reasons to come here: the cathedral of Bari conserves the remains of St. Nicholas (yes, Virginia, there is a Santa Claus); Pope Francis just canonized the martyrs of Otranto in 2013; every small town or city alike has its patron saint with festive week-long celebrations leading up to his/her feast day; and its Holy Week processions -- rich in tradition and pageantry -- attract people from all over Italy and beyond.

However, the most important pilgrimage destination in Apulia is without a doubt the Gargano Mountains -- known as the "spur" of the Italian boot that juts into the Adriatic Sea. In the early Middle Ages, St. Michael the Archangel appeared in a grotto four times in what is now the town of Monte Sant'Angelo. Its position overlooking the Adriatic Sea at the end of the ancient Roman road, the Via Appia Antica, made it an important stopover point for medieval pilgrims and crusaders alike journeying back and forth between the Holy Land and Italy.

Today, however, there is a new saint in those same Gargano Mountains: St. Pio of Pietrelcina. It all began on that fateful September 20, 1918 morning when this young Capuchin friar received the five wounds of Christ in a simple hermitage on the outskirts of a poor mountain village. Word spread like wildfire among illiterate peasants and sophisticated intelligentsia alike. They heard about a mystical priest who could read souls, prophesy, bi-locate, and speak with the Virgin Mary, Jesus, angels and the saints.

From that moment onward, people began coming to the remote town of San Giovanni Rotondo by the multitudes. They walked for days or traveled in primitive automobiles along unpaved, potholed roads. Many were suffering from serious illnesses and hoped for a healing for themselves or for a loved one; others were racked with guilt and wanted to make their confession or hear him say Mass; some were just plain curious or nosy; and still others were superstitious and wanted to take a piece of his cord or habit home with them. Yet all hoped to experience something special, even supernatural, from this mystical *Alter Christus*.

And still today -- almost fifty years after the death of the saint -- little has changed. Some five million people continue to come to San Giovanni Rotondo each year on pilgrimage. And they still come for the same reasons as when he was still alive. People have heeded Padre Pio's words when he said, "After my death I will do more. My real mission will begin after my death."

In fact, devotion to the stigmatized saint throughout the region -- indeed in all of Italy -- is stronger than ever. His face is everywhere. You see him in the region's ubiquitous roadside shrines (known as *edicole*) as well as in statues in churches. Icons of Padre Pio adorn people's living rooms and bedrooms as well as the walls of restaurants and coffee bars. You'll even see images of him in automotive garages, public schools, and on the side of tractor trailers traversing the peninsula's highways. Everyone here knows and loves Padre Pio.

And this is the native region of Adolfo Affatato. Over sixty years ago, he, too, once set out along the primitive roads from Foggia to San Giovanni Rotondo to get a glimpse of Padre Pio. Yet, he was not there as a devotee; he, too, was curious. He was just sixteen years old -- little more than a boy -- and he had heard of this mysterious Capuchin "monk" who could read souls. He was there, quite frankly, because he wanted to know if this "soul reader" could tell him if he had passed his high school final exams. Yet, unbeknownst to this naive boy, this short encounter was about to radically transform his life.

The evening prayer service had just finished and Padre Pio was making his way through the crowded sacristy to return to his cell to retire for the night. Adolfo was there, too, watching curiously at a distance among the packed crowds and sweltering July heat. He watched carefully as this pained, stooped-over, stigmatized saint passed by. Suddenly -- as when Jesus called his disciples according to a divine logic not understood by man -- Padre Pio chose this young boy. To his amazement (and that of everyone else standing nearby) Padre Pio suddenly stopped, turned toward him and said, "*Adolfo, vieni qui*" ("Adolfo, come here.")

That was the first of Adolfo's countless visits to San Giovanni Rotondo to see Padre Pio. Soon after, Padre Pio accepted Adolfo as his "spiritual son": a special relationship limited to very few carefully selected people. From then on, Adolfo began keeping a diary in which he journaled about his experiences with the saint and what he witnessed.

Some forty-five years later, Adolfo and several other still living spiritual sons of Padre Pio were reminiscing about *Il Padre* ("The Father" -- the way they affectionately refer to Padre Pio) when Adolfo mentioned his diary. One of them told Adolfo that the time had come in which he needed to tell people about his experiences with Padre Pio saying, "You don't realize the good you can do for so many people." Adolfo knew he would not be around much longer and he decided to to let the world know who *il Padre* was to him. Thus, in 2008, Adolfo published the first edition of his book with the title, "*Io e Il Padre*" ("The Father and I").

Adolfo initially considered publishing his experiences with Padre Pio as a simple diary. Yet, in the end, he chose to make it into a book in order to give the reader more information about Padre Pio. As such, his thoughts and the stories tend to jump around somewhat sporadically. But for the author, it doesn't matter. Because the book has but one goal... in fact, Adolfo Affatato has one mission in life: to make Padre Pio known "more and better."

Southern Italians are generally known for their kindness and hospitality. Yet I found Adolfo to be extraordinarily generous. The first time we met, he gave me a wonderful framed photograph of Padre Pio, and then he promptly loaded up my trunk with freshly baked breads, cheeses, and local pasta from Apulia. He also treated me to a delicious three-course seafood lunch. (Our second meeting was much the same). When I talk to him on the phone, I always customarily ask him how he is doing. And I always get the same response -- a quote from Psalm 131: "As quiet and serene as a child in his mother's arms."

Adolfo is confident in his mission, and for the past ten years he has been traveling all over Italy tirelessly carrying it out. And lately, he has been very busy. He gives conferences on Padre Pio to audiences consisting of a few dozen people or a couple thousand. But he doesn't waste time counting them. He speaks to one person or one thousand equally passionately. When he talks about Padre Pio, his eyes twinkle with wonder, he chokes up, and he is visibly moved.

Several years ago, he received some notoriety when he appeared on the respected and popular prime-time Italian talk show, "*Porta a Porta*" ("Door to Door"). Just recently, he was interviewed at length for the major Italian network, Rai 2, by a Vatican priest-journalist for a special edition on Padre Pio as the saint's body will be moved into the basilica of St. Peter's in Rome for one week during this year's Extraordinary Jubilee Year of Mercy. And just last week, Adolfo gave a conference to the priests of the diocese of Naples on the theme of Padre Pio and mercy having been invited personally by the cardinal of Naples himself. This is just a sample of how Adolfo, now seventy-nine years old, spends his time.

Yet, despite all of this, Adolfo is by no means prideful. Even though he was personally chosen by Padre Pio for an important mission and he witnessed numerous extraordinary events involving Padre Pio (which he has published here in English for the first time), the author never boasts or tries to impress the reader. Instead, everything he says or does is faithful to his mission: to make Padre Pio known "more and better."

In our first telephone conversation, Adolfo told me several times that he did not write his book for any profit whatsoever. The second time we talked, he told me how he did not write his book for any profit at all. The third time we talked, he told me yet again how he did not write this book for any profit whatsoever. The fourth time we talked, he asked me if I understood why he wrote this book. I told him, "I know it's not for profit." He said, "You are correct. If I had chosen to, I could have become rich 'commercializing' my relationship with Padre Pio. But instead, I chose to personally pay out of my own pocket for the full cost of the printing of both editions of my book. And when I give away my books, I always ask people to make an offering directly to the friars in San Giovanni Rotondo who have several foundations for the poor. Further, I always personally pay for all my hotel and travel expenses when I give conferences on Padre Pio. And I do this because this book has one objective: to make Padre Pio known more and better in his humanity and his divinity. This is the why I do what I do: to give back a little of what I received." Adolfo is clearly a man who "walks the walk" and would certainly make Padre Pio proud for choosing him to be his spiritual son.

Professionally, Adolfo was never a friar, a theologian, or an academic. Instead, he was a successful businessman and insurance underwriter. Married with two (now grown) children, he lived his life under the spiritual direction of Padre Pio, which he credits as the reason for all his professional success.

Despite the fact that he never took one theology course and the author's own statement that he is a "simple layman," his religious formation is profound. In fact, his book provides a remarkable framework for understanding the spirituality of Padre Pio. Rather than auditing theological lectures in a classroom, Adolfo had the fortune of sitting at Padre Pio's side listening to this great saint (who spoke predominantly "the language of silence," in the words of the author). And after spending a lifetime reflecting on what he saw and heard, he offers uncanny insight into the mystical and supernatural phenomena surrounding the great saint's life.

Despite his lack of theological degrees or certificates, however, the author is quite familiar with Scripture, the lives of the saints, and the Church Fathers -- all of which he frequently cites and quotes. Furthermore, for "a simple layman," he wades into fairly deep theological waters. He does a great job describing what the theological concept of "divinization" looks like without ever mentioning the word (*theosis* in Greek; see CCC: 460, 1988). He also offers frequent reflections on the Incarnation, man's nature as being both corporeal and spiritual, sacrificial and intercessory suffering, and contemplative prayer -- again without ever using theological terms.

In the end, imprimaturs, academic jargon, or theological paradigms are not important to the author. What is important to him is simply giving back the love he received from his beloved spiritual father and in the process making him known "better and more."

Adolfo feels a personal responsibility to teach everyone he meets about the lessons he learned personally and directly from Padre Pio. And he does so in a way that is pragmatic, useful, and hands-on. Thus, he shows the reader a practical method of living the Christian life. And everything Adolfo learned from Padre Pio is right here in this text. It is chock-full of spiritual lessons ranging from the necessity to be grateful and prayerful, as well as living one's life charitably for others. Thus, his book (and life) is highly evangelical.

And Adolfo was able to do all this because Padre Pio showed him the face of Christ... in addition to His crucified body. Through the intercession of Padre Pio, Adolfo Affatato ultimately encountered Jesus Christ Himself. And in that encounter, he learned about Christ's Heart which is full of all-encompassing love for "a sinful and suffering humanity."

The book that follows is fascinating as the author recounts new stories about the supernatural side of Padre Pio as witnessed firsthand by the author. It is touching and moving as the author reveals the tender and endearing side of Padre Pio. Yet, ultimately, what emerges is the heartfelt story of a man who loved Padre Pio intimately as his own father, and in turn, discovered Christ.

In the end, this book is the fruit of what Padre Pio once told Adolfo, "Give the love that I have put into your heart to those to whom you draw near, because in this is the meaning of life." This book, indeed Adolfo's entire life, is a response to that personal mandate he received directly from Padre Pio.

Clearly, the love that Adolfo received from Padre Pio (which he had received from Jesus Christ) is here in this book for all to receive. And this is simply so that you, the reader, can develop or deepen your own relationship with this great intercessor in order to receive similar blessings from Jesus Christ through the great stigmatized saint of Pietrelcina.

Just before his death, Padre Pio said, "I belong to everyone. Now everyone can say: 'Padre Pio is mine.'" Therefore, Padre Pio is not limited to those fortunate spiritual sons and daughters who were blessed to be able to sit at his side. Now, glorified in heaven, anyone can be blessed by the life of Padre Pio, which is ultimately the blessing of Christ Himself. And in this book -- and in his life -- Adolfo Affatato shows the way.

Bret Thoman, OFS

Translator's notes:

I added some information that was not in the original Italian to clarify or enhance the text. Whenever I did so, I put it in brackets. I also sometimes added contextual information to clarify the text, which I preceded with "Tr.:" (i.e. translator).

The author frequently refers to Padre Pio affectionately as "Il Padre," which means "The Father." I have translated it throughout the text simply as "Padre."

Note that 100% of the proceeds from sales of this book will go to a charity or foundation, as designated by the author, Adolfo Affatato.

THE ENCOUNTER

It all began in July, 1953. The air in Foggia was already so hot that locals were seeking refuge either at the beach or up in the hills. The infamous Favonius was blowing -- that warm African wind out of the south that makes life in my native city brutal.

At the time, I was completing high school (having studied accounting) and I, too, decided to head for the hills of San Giovanni Rotondo. I did so not so much in search of the town's gentler air, as much for the fact that some friends had told me about a friar named Padre Pio who could read people's souls and foresee the future. Therefore, my first encounter was one born solely out of curiosity… and especially to know if I had passed my final exams.

Once I arrived in San Giovanni Rotondo, I was just in time for the service of the Exposition of the Blessed Sacrament. As the small church was packed to capacity, it offset every benefit offered by the cool air just outside.

I witnessed the entire service and was struck by the intensity of the spiritual atmosphere. And when I heard Padre Pio's voice, interrupted by tears, recite the prayer of St. Alphonsus to the Virgin, I was deeply moved.

After the service, I withdrew to the small sacristy. It, too, was packed with the faithful and was hot. Nonetheless, I was able to find some space -- rather uncomfortable -- in the rear to stand. I remained there if for nothing else just to have the satisfaction of watching Padre Pio pass by.

The corridor the faithful left in the center to allow Padre Pio to return to his cell was so narrow that the people on either side were almost touching one another. Finally, after the customary ritual, he began to move with his heavy steps toward the door on the left to return inside the friary enclosure. Halfway there, however, he stopped, turned around, looked in my direction and said, "Adolfo,

11

come here."

At that moment, I thought he was referring to anyone other than me as the privileged one. This was the first time I had ever visited San Giovanni Rotondo and I had never met Padre Pio before. So I stood completely still.

Yet he repeated himself saying, "Adolfo, come here." At that point, given his insistence together with the fact that no one else went forward, I said from afar, "Eh, Padre, did you call me?" And he responded somewhat wryly, "Is my name Adolfo?"

So I made my way through the throng of people toward him. Once I reached him, Padre Pio said to me, "I have been waiting for you for a long time." He then put his hand on my head and continued walking toward the cloister.

There are not words to describe what I felt at that moment. I can only say that my first encounter was full of joy and inner peace. In front of me, I witnessed a man who radiated so much light. Immediately the episode of St. Paul on the road to Damascus came to mind [Cf. Acts 9:3-9].

Everyone present peppered me with questions, but I clearly did not know how to answer them. I told everyone that it was the first time I had ever seen Padre Pio. Yet this only increased the disbelief of those present -- as well as my realization that I was in the presence of someone, something, truly extraordinary. I also realized immediately that I had been called, predestined, without merit.

> Padre Pio said to me, "I have been waiting for you for a long time..."
>
> Everyone peppered me with questions. I told everyone that it was the first time I had ever seen Padre Pio.

My life was totally changed. And from that moment on, every day has been accompanied by the constant presence of Padre Pio.

I did not see in him a man, Francesco Forgione, who became a friar taking the name, Padre Pio; instead I saw him as a spiritual being, a wonderful spiritual being. Certainly it is not easy to describe the emotions I felt when in his presence. When you experience such extraordinary events, you lose track of your surroundings and what's going on around you, and you feel carried away by the wonderment to the point that it can seem as if it were an ordinary event.

Then there is another consideration to make: I was very young then, with a cheerful character and an appealing friendliness. This caused me to be too open and direct with Padre, which, looking back now many years later, I certainly would not do today. Because it was only after his death when I understood the importance of those experiences with Padre and of the extraordinary event that happened to me. And, for this, I will never tire of giving thanks to the Lord. I was the recipient -- the witness -- of so many extraordinary events before which words are insignificant and the mind is too small to fully take in what he himself said, "I am a mystery even to myself."

> "I am a mystery
> even to myself."
> --Padre Pio

The way in which we live our spirituality determines our true fulfillment on earth as children of God. Only by living in harmony with the divine will can we ensure that all His Omnipotence will be embodied within us. And this is exactly what happened to Padre Pio.

Each day we move and act constantly within an invisible sea of thoughts and intentions. God will always give us what we ask for when it serves our internal growth based on our faith.

Padre Pio was sent to earth to witness to the love of God and His Omnipotence which can do all things, as well as to be an instrument of countless miracles.

Padre Pio expressed so much affection every time we met.

13

Adolfo pointing out the exact location in 1953 Padre Pio called him by name out of a group of people. Adolfo and Padre Pio had never met prior to that day.

MY FIRST CONFESSION

Padre Pio was like a consuming fire that attracted everything to himself. He was a refined hunter of souls and he had a method all his own to conquer each one. Once he took hold of someone's heart, he would penetrate it, turn it inside out, empty it of all sin, and fully take possession of it as the stigmatized representative of Christ, giver of life.

So, after a few months of visiting him regularly and learning from him -- months in which I felt more and more attracted to the light that emanated from his face -- I scheduled an appointment to go to confession. It was the first confession I made with Padre.

You can imagine my excitement at finding myself alone with Padre, even if it was just for a few minutes. It was so extraordinary it did not seem real. This is how it went,

Padre Pio: "Praised be Jesus Christ."

Me: "May he always be praised."

Padre Pio: "So, how long has it been since your last confession?"

Me: Dead silence… I was so tense, my excitement so great, that I couldn't remember a thing.

Padre Pio: "Well, so you've lost your tongue? What did you come here for? To waste my time? Do you not see how many people are outside waiting?"

Me: "Father, I don't remember anything."

Padre Pio: "Okay, so now I'll help you. The last time you confessed was in the church of Jesus and Mary and you confessed to Father Bonaventure. So, what sins have you committed since then?"

Me: Still silence. I was captivated by his eyes and I took delight in that vast light. I was continually touching his arm and I became intoxicated by that peculiar fragrance that emanated from his crucified hands. I said, "Padre, I no longer remember anything."

Padre Pio then said, "Then I will tell you what you have committed." And one by one he listed all the sins I was most guilty of. He then said, "My son, if you keep this up, do you know what will happen to you? You will end up under the feet of St. Michael. And do you know who is there? Your friend, the devil."

> And one by one he listed all the sins I was most guilty of.

In his fatherly love, he understood my condition and he absolved me. However, he required me to do my penance in the grotto of Saint Michael. [Tr.: Saint Michael the Archangel appeared in Monte Sant'Angelo, about 25 km. {15 miles} from San Giovanni Rotondo, several times as early as the fifth century AD; since then, it has been an important Christian place of devotion.]

Thus what had already happened to so many others now happened to me: my recently conquered soul became a creature of his. And now he would follow and protect me as one of his dear children. In fact, he once said, "I will be at the gates of paradise until the last of my children enters."

Traumatized by this first experience, a few months passed before I reserved for confession a second time. This time, however, seven days before my appointment, I confessed to another priest. So when I was called go to confession, I went happily. This time I was certain that at least I would avoid looking bad again.

When Padre asked me what sins I had committed, I responded that I did not think I had done anything really wrong -- just a few lies, no harm. Yet, I received the following response, "So, you came here to waste my time? Do you not see how many people are waiting?" It was practically the same response I had gotten the first time, only this time it was for different reasons.

At that moment my eyes met his. I could not resist and in a burst of affection I told him, "Father, I love you so much, I would prefer to never have to leave you." Suddenly his large eyes filled with tears, and, visibly moved, he said, "Obviously you do not know the love that I have for you." Today, after more than fifty years, it's as if these words had been written in blood on my heart.

He gave me absolution, then paused and added, "Take that chair and sit down over there in the corner; when I finish [hearing confessions], accompany me upstairs." When Father Giustino saw me sitting there, he asked me to get up and move. Even though I said I had been authorized by Padre, he would not listen to my explanation. In the meantime, Padre was hearing someone else's confession. As soon as he finished, he beckoned to a fellow friar and said to him, "Leave him there, he's not bothering anyone." This was one of the most beautiful displays of affection I ever received from Padre. And after all these years, I am still moved at the memory.

I still fully feel all his love that surrounds me and guides me along my life journey. Wherever I happen to be, I always speak of him with all the affection of a son who received so much. And in all those to whom I speak, I sow the seed of love toward this enormous saint within the Church, this living crucifix who walked among us.

My great admiration and love for Padre increased more and more each day, especially when I realized that it was he himself who asked God to be crucified out of love for the Almighty and for the salvation of humanity so that all people could find in him a certain orientation of faith and prayer. Therefore, I was able to ascertain how, in the ocean of thoughts that envelops the universe, Padre's desire passed from hiddenness to openness through the manifestation of the signs of the crucifixion on his body.

Therefore, with his life of prayer, obedience and suffering, he became a channel through which all divine grace flowed freely and abundantly in him, which he then put at the disposal of all those who turned to him pleading for graces and intercessions. He had become a wellspring of miracles for all those who needed them.

One day after the women's confession, a lady with a northern Italian accent approached him while I was standing there and pleaded for her daughter who was very ill. He listened and then reached into his tunic, took out a medal, gave it to her, and assured her of his prayers. When he closed the door to return to his cell, he said to me along the way, "That woman is now convinced that it is I who will work this miracle; however, I'm just a friar who prays, God does the rest." And how can God not relent when faced with a mother's pleas? I understood that he would intercede for that poor woman. Yet I never found out what eventually happened because I never saw this woman again.

The near-sighted philosophies of positivism and scientism of the twentieth century led to the triumph of reason, which does not allow for extraordinary events which simply require belief through mere faith -- events that invite us to direct our thoughts upward toward heaven. Today, our brutish humanity has often lost the habit of lifting our eyes upward and discerning that the divine is right there alongside us and we don't even realize it.

Padre Pio lived for more than eighty years. He spoke to us; he taught us to pray; he offered a heroic witness of the Christian life; and he worked miracles that defied reason. And yet men have remained largely indifferent. Only a few had the pleasure of ever knowing him, and fewer still were those chosen and privileged to become his spiritual children. If humanity had realized all this, certainly the faithful and Padre's children would be in the tens of millions.

Since his death, the number of believers has grown incredibly. Consider that each year more than seven million pilgrims visit his tomb. They are attracted to something they cannot explain, and they seek an inner peace they invariably find.

Modern man has lost sight of his spiritual heritage; Padre Pio, however, totally immersed himself in prayer where he received God's message and his longing for God was satisfied. As one breath follows the next, so his speech was a continual succession of Rosaries -- one Ave Maria after the other. He recited fifty rosaries a day! This was God's language; this was the daily dialogue between Padre Pio and God.

This is the sweetest Padre Pio -- crucified in his heart, hands, side and feet with his face reflecting the archway of heaven.

Accompanying Padre Pio to the entrance of his cell.

This is Padre Pio's confessional that Adolfo used in 1953. Padre Pio sat in the chair to the right. This one is now protected by a glass enclosure. The women used a different confessional in the main area of the church.

SPIRITUAL CHILD

Padre had numerous gifts: prophecy, reading souls, bilocation, emitting fragrance (even from a distance) and working miracles. His bleeding wounds could easily have inflated his pride. Instead, he found refuge in humility, obedience, and in his fabricated mask of gruffiness which hid his enormous heart. The halo of the supernatural about him did not in the least take away his behavior as a simple and common man. The words said about Moses could equally apply to him, "Now the man Moses was very humble, more than anyone else on earth" [Numbers 12:3].

In the wake of the many gifts he received, it would be logical to assume that people could have had doubts about his mental state. Yet the Lord appreciated His beloved son, and while He made him seem like one of us, He also made Padre Pio a dispenser of graces.

Given my disposition, I found a natural harmony with my spiritual director, with whom by then I could no longer do without. Therefore, one day after confession, I asked Padre if I could be his spiritual child. He looked at me pleased and happily replied: "Of course I accept you as my son. Why do you think I told you I had been waiting for you for so long? I was waiting for this moment. But remember, don't make me look bad... Instead, be a worthy son, because the world is tired of words. It needs examples."

Only God knows the joy I felt in my heart that day -- I felt happy and gladness. His eyes were so beautiful and penetrating they descended into the depths of my soul. By then, I had my "investiture," and I was ready to face the world with my new "business card."

> "...be a worthy son, because the world is tired of words. It needs examples."
> --Padre Pio

21

I do not know exactly how many of us [spiritual children] there were then. Surely we were not many, because Padre was very selective. Even today, after fifty years, we are still relatively few. But this only makes our responsibility increase. In fact, one day Professor Enrico Medi said: "Dear friend, future generations will envy us for the many privileges we received." [Tr.: Enrico Medi was a scientist and spiritual son of Padre Pio. After his death in 1974, he was declared Servant of God. A beatification process is currently underway.]

I understood that Padre Pio had the purpose of his life through continual suffering, prayer, and daily meditation on the crucified Jesus: dispensing love for all. And where love reigns there are always miracles. Michel de Montaigne once said, "The great and glorious masterpiece of man is living for a purpose. When this goal is contained in serving God and neighbor, behold the creed of those who are able to perform miracles."

As each day passed, my knowledge of Padre became more and more refined. And this only increased more and more my affection at being his spiritual child. And I did everything to honor this coveted recognition.

Today I can say that I do not know what I would have become without having known and been directed by Padre Pio. He always guided me toward the right choices at the right time. It was wonderful to be able to ask, "Padre, what should I do?" And he always had the right answer. Indeed many times he wouldn't let me finish my sentence, "It's useless to get all worked up. First, finish the course on Public Law." [Tr.: Many departments in Italian universities require basic law courses as part of the core curriculum.]

As I continue to write, I'm now beginning to realize that this book is more than a simple diary; it's an authentic little book in which I'm attempting to use my own inadequate words to offer various considerations about Padre. I have read many books published about Padre -- many solely for commercial purposes -- especially by people who never knew him. The ones written by Father Alessandro da Ripabottoni are excellent; those written by Renzo Allegri and Rino Cammilleri are also good.

But, dear friend who is reading my book, believe me, the idea that we have of Padre Pio -- we who knew him and were fortunate enough to be near him -- is different. Something remains inside you that time can never erase. I say this only because I am aware that my words cannot adequately describe the size and scope of this giant who revolutionized the twentieth century. Perhaps only those who come after us -- after reading his letters and the documents in the Capuchin archives -- will be able to deliver to history a more complete picture than what has been done to date.

I, like so many other spiritual children, still have a vivid memory of what it was like to be blessed in the light of his presence. So to leave something of value on paper, all we have to do is to take recourse to photographic documentation… which reminds me that it all happened. This is why -- before the unstoppable law of time diminishes the memories of those unforgettable moments -- I must leave them written on these pages for my children, relatives and friends to always remember how fortunate I was. I am indebted, strongly indebted, with my life. And when you finish reading these pages, I think that you, too, will agree with me how much divine attention this simple man [the author] received.

And, speaking of spiritual children, the one person who left a profound memory on me is Professor Medi. He was a great scientist, a man of prayer, a great orator who charmed audiences, and a devoted lover of Our Lady. When Padre Pio retired to his cell -- and one night I was there, too -- Professor Medi would bow his head and ask for a blessing. Once, when Padre Pio passed by, the superior, Father Carmelo from Sessano, asked him, "Professor, why do you, a spiritual son who is so intimate with Padre, lower your head?" And Medi responded without hesitating, "Because I am not worthy to look at the face of Jesus."

Professor Medi offered the following definition of Padre Pio, "Padre represents the naturalness of the supernatural." This is the best definition that has ever been stated about Padre Pio and one that expresses his true nature. Yes, because for him prophesy, working miracles, and speaking with Our Lady were the most natural things in this world. In fact, Padre once responded to his confessor after he had asked him, "Padre, but do you actually talk to the Madonna?" Surprised, Padre responded, "But why? You don't talk to her?"

He emanated a superhuman energy deep within his persona. It was a powerful and invisible force that could be perceived by anyone who drew near him, and he brought all those who entered within his spiritual world. The way he looked and spoke was profound, illuminated. Everything seemed directly inspired by God.

Despite their differences, people inherently possess the same desires. They have the same heartbeat that unites them to the one God -- the same God who crucified Padre Pio as an example of sanctified pain at the service of a suffering humanity. The same Padre Pio who -- with stoicism and regal dignity -- bore the signs of the stigmata. He bore the wounds as if he did not have them. Yet, he suffered so deeply as if they were constantly being renewed. They were "unspeakable pain" as he once described them to another friar.

He never shunned people stopping by for a moment,
even just to say, "Good night, Father."

ADMISSION OF SUFFERING

Padre Pio found relief in the vision that awaited him at the end of his earthly journey toward heaven. There his sanctified body would gravitate in a wonderful level of peace, love and infinite joy in a magnificent world of boundless beauty, and everything would radiate light and would be coordinated in a perfect order from a single source of light radiating love -- that infinite and divine love that embraces everything. All this allowed him to endure serenely his "daily tortures," as he himself referred to them.

One evening I was a fortunate witness of all this. At the end of the evening service, after spending time in the sitting area with some other spiritual children, Padre retired to his cell accompanied by Father Onorato. As usual, I followed him in. Once inside his cell, I remained near the door. He sat on the chair and continued to pray while Father Onorato untied his sandals so he could rest his feet on the stool. At that moment, a strange paleness came over his face and he grimaced in pain.

> With a deep and cavernous voice that manifested all his suffering, he replied, "Only I know the pain I feel."

Father Onorato immediately asked him, "Padre, do [your wounds] hurt?" With a deep and cavernous voice that manifested all his suffering, he replied, "Only I know the pain I feel. Yet, the Lord permits it so I do not become proud of the gifts I have received, and to remind me of my human nature."

Father Onorato -- who was always close to Padre, accustomed to his way of speaking and who knew of the extraordinary and supernatural -- was at that moment intent on placing him in the most comfortable position. Perhaps he did not pay much attention to Padre's words. I, on the other hand, was taken aback. It was as if he had directed those words to me so I would not forget them.

I said good night to him, closed the door, and set out to return home. Halfway down the hallway, however, I had a strong desire to return and say goodbye to him again. So I went back.

I opened the door and said, "Father, I would like to wish you a good night." And he responded, "But didn't we already say goodbye to one another?" Yet he sensed my outpouring of affection and beckoned me to approach him. He put his hand on my head, blessed me and said, "Holy night to you, too." How beautiful was that evening! Now I could go home happy.

For future reference, as soon as I arrived home, I wrote down Padre's sentence which was already written in my heart. It was a great phrase -- one of the greatest I ever heard from Padre. It demonstrated the essentially spiritual nature that trudged his tormented human body throughout his earthly pilgrimage. In fact, that evening represented a significant turning point for me.

At that point, I discovered one of the many mysteries of Padre and [why] so many extraordinary events took place in his presence on a daily basis. In fact, some time earlier, Father Lino Barbato had told me that during a moment of ecstasy -- the word I use to describe those long colloquies that took place in his cell -- Padre Pio told a fellow friar about something he had told Jesus. Looking up to Jesus, he said, "If You give Your consent, I will be actor and spectator at the same time of all You shall do in me as if done by me."

So this is how to explain the intentionally abrupt manner with which he responded when he sensed the danger (which continuously presented itself) of gestures of fanaticism bordering on idolatry by those who saw him as the author of miracles. This is why he readily replied to all, "But what do you want from me? I'm just a friar who prays." And all the while only he conserved the great secret in his heart: that of being a channel through which all God's grace flowed -- the true cause of all supernatural events attributed to him.

Padre Pio had given everything to God in a life of prayer and suffering, and God filled him with many gifts. "To live is to give, to give is divine" to allow the divine fire that burned in his heart to radiate externally. His life was a continuous giving of himself to those who suffered and to all those he freed from sin to deliver into the hands of God cleansed.

Thus, the sentence that was repeated to me by Padre Pio was nothing more than the confirmation of his full awareness that every time he interceded for someone, only with difficulty would God not satisfy him. As the poet once said, "And nothing to such an intercessor will be denied" [cf. Torquato Tasso, "Jerusalem Delivered" 2, 52].

He did all this completely naturally. It was as if working a miracle were the simplest thing to do in the world. And he never tired of giving thanks to God for having made him a dispenser of graces.

GRATITUDE

Gratitude was very important to him. One evening I asked him, "Padre, what is the sin that God forgives with difficulty?" He responded: "God forgives everything. But there is one sin that He forgives only with great difficulty: humanity's ingratitude from birth to death." God, in His omnipotence, becomes impotent only before humanity from whom He asks for just a little bit of love. But He knows how to wait.

Just think for a moment how much we can reflect on this answer: God creates His most perfect creation -- His masterpiece -- humanity made in His image and likeness. Yet, out of respect of humanity's free will, He waits for His creation to remember the Creator of his life.

Here, in my opinion, emerges one of the tasks entrusted to Padre Pio by God: to bring back so many lost sheep into the fold as a sure beacon guiding all to find the peace and inner serenity they've lost. Today the sheepfold is indeed larger. In fact, it may not even be possible to count just how many people have been converted by the life and example of Padre Pio.

> "God forgives everything. But there is one sin that He forgives only with great difficulty: humanity's ingratitude from birth to death."
> --Padre Pio

PADRE'S MASS

Finally, the day arrived when it was my turn to serve Mass alongside Padre. Usually this privilege was reserved for a friar along with one or two of his spiritual children. I will never forget the excitement I felt as I stood by his side at the altar.

You can imagine the emotions and feelings that filled my heart for my first Mass. In fact, I didn't sleep a wink the night before. As a young and unworthy man, I was at Padre's side during the most glorious moment of his long day -- the celebration of the Mass. The Mass was the key to understanding his mission as a priest who offered himself as a victim and where he offered all the requests that came to him from all over the world at the throne of the Most High.

I arrived so early for my first Mass that the church was still closed. Later, when it was time, I went into the sacristy, and thanks to Father Carmelo I went up to wait for Padre to come out of his cell. The door was opened and Padre -- with his heavenly face and nearly hoarse voice -- said immediately in a deep tone: "Praised be Jesus Christ."

After the ritual of donning his liturgical vestments, we set out toward the altar. My excitement was so great that my legs were trembling lightly. Finally, the celebration began and I felt as if I had been transported into another world. I was attracted by the divine light that emanated from Padre's sanctified body.

First of all, I should say that Padre Pio would begin his Mass at 4:30 AM It was at that hour, in the most profound silence of the friary, interrupted only by his coughing -- that nasty cough that never left him in peace -- when he began his long meticulous preparation to encounter his beloved Jesus and re-live with Him the entire ordeal of Golgotha.

Usually, there was space on one side of the altar reserved for Pietruccio [Little Peter] -- a blind man who had been close to Padre since his youth. Faced with the

31

question of whether or not he preferred the sight of his soul or that of his body, he chose the sight of his soul. And from that moment on, he became a beloved son of Padre Pio. To the amazement of all, he moved about the friary freely, as if guided by some invisible figure. But the most amazing thing is that every time I spoke with Pietruccio, it was he who comforted me; a serenity and inner peace difficult to explain radiated from his voice.

On the other side of the altar was often the petite figure of Sir Battisti, the administrator of the hospital, House for the Relief of Suffering. He was always seen kneeling throughout the entire Mass in total concentration. [Tr.: Padre Pio initiated and founded a hospital and medical-research center in San Giovanni Rotondo known as the *Casa Sollievo della Sofferenza* {Home for the Relief of the Suffering}. Today it is one of the most important hospitals in Southern Italy.

Padre Pio with Carlo Campanini in his sitting room.

The church was packed and overflowing with the faithful who came from all over. People began lining up outside the door at 3:00 AM braving the cold, the rain, and the biting wind to have a chance to be able to sit in the front row. After people raced in to get the best seats and the commotion passed, total silence descended upon the entire church. Neither breath nor murmur could be heard as the crowd immersed themselves in prayer to prepare for Padre's entrance.

They were intense and fitful moments. Then the bell would ring at 4:30 announcing the beginning of the Holy Mass. And finally, Padre came out of the sacristy with his typical lumbering and heavy steps as his feet -- pierced by the crucifixion -- caused him so much pain. And then Mass began.

It was immediately apparent that his Mass was not like any other. As soon as they saw Padre, many of the faithful would become emotional and begin weeping. Some pleaded to him out loud while others, starry-eyed, whispered softly to Padre. There was a spiritual feeling between the people of God and the victim who offered himself there on Calvary.

While serving Padre Pio at Mass, I witnessed him transformed. The color of his face would change from a striking paleness to a light, almost celestial, pink. He would sometimes shake his head as if attempting to drive "someone" or "something" away who was annoying him. For long stretches during the celebration, his eyes would remain nearly closed as if blinded by a dazzling light in front of him.

And then there was the consecration of the Host. During those long moments, his gaze would become like stone. He would repeat over and over with his voice interrupted by tears, saying, "Lord I am not worthy." Now the sacrifice was finished -- the victim had given himself up for the redemption of many sinners. It was the price that had to be paid to ransom at least in part the great love of God. It was truly the crucifixion of Christ repeating itself.

All this is in clear contrast with so many noisy Masses I hear today accompanied by guitars and drums which only make it difficult for the faithful to have the necessary silent preparation to receive the consecrated Host.

We arrived at the lavabo and when I picked up the ewer to pour water over Padre's fingertips, I instinctively began staring at the center of the palms of his hands. Before the Mass, Padre Pio had removed his gloves with the fingers cut off, and this was my only opportunity to look at his stigmata.

I observed the wounds very well: there was a hole in the center of his hands, and all around the wound was covered in blood. But what impressed me the most was the color of the blood -- it was a fresh red. It did not seem as though he had had them for forty years.

As soon as he noticed that I was observing his stigmata, he said, "Hey kid, mind your own business." I quickly came to my senses, and with a nod, as if to apologize, I completed the ritual hand-washing and went back to my place.

33

When the Mass ended, we returned to the sacristy. After we all said in unison, "*Prosit, Padre*," he turned around and said to me, "You, come over here." So I approached him and he said, "Did you hear Mass?" I responded, "What do you mean, Father? I was there serving you." Then he said with a severe face, "No! You looked at things that were not yours. Now go hear another Mass." Then, with a paternal smile, he added, "My son, these are things you cannot understand."

Thus ended my first exalting Mass with Padre.

During the celebration of my wedding (April 23, 1966)

MARQUISE BOSCHI

I graduated from high school in 1957. As I did in all my major life events, I told Padre that I had enrolled at the University of Naples. Let me start by saying that the economic situation of my family was modest. My father was a city employee, and he frequently worried about how he would care for a family of ten children. Nevertheless, with numerous sacrifices, I was able to sign up to study Economics and Business.

While speaking with Padre, he asked me, "Do you know where you will go yet? Have you found a place to stay?" I replied, "No Padre, I do not know yet." He then called Padre Carmelo from Sessano, the Superior of the friary, and told him, "Take Adolfo to Marquise Boschi in Naples so she can find him accommodations so he can study." [Tr.: A marquise is a noblewoman with the rank of marquess or the wife of a marquess.]

After we decided on the day of departure, we arrived in Naples at the Marquise's villa which was in Posillipo. [Tr.: The hill district of Posillipo, on the waterfront Gulf of Naples, is one of the most prestigious and scenic districts of Naples.] She was overjoyed at seeing Father Carmelo, and was just as happy upon learning of Padre Pio's request to help me. Father Carmelo then celebrated Mass in her private chapel. After offering us tea and cookies, the Marquise phoned a boarding school for orphans -- one of the many charities where she served as president.

And so I found housing in a building run by ENAOLI (National Entity for Assistance of Orphans of Italian Workers) off Piazza San Gaetano in downtown Naples. My job would be to tutor the many orphans who were housed there. I practically lived in the church of San Lorenzo Maggiore, a monument with important historical and architectural value.

Once again, Padre showed me so much love and care for me as if he were my real father.

Many times I had the privilege of praying with him in the small choir area where the stigmata occurred.

SEND ME YOUR GUARDIAN ANGEL

Despite my move, my life did not change very much. Economic possibilities permitting, I went home almost every week in order to go to San Giovanni Rotondo. [Tr.: Distance of 180 km.] And I must say that my visits became more prominent in the period around exam time so that I could commend myself to Padre's prayers.

And so it was that one day Padre told me, "My son, you don't need to come all the way out here. As often as you need to, enter any church and send me your guardian angel." And so I did from that time onward... That is, until the day I had to sit for my Private Law examination.

This particular exam had me deeply worried. In fact, it was not uncommon for students to have to take it three or four times to pass it. So that morning I left my room earlier than usual and visited at least five churches. And each time, I sent my guardian angel to Padre. Also, from my first examination onward, I had the custom of inserting a picture of Padre Pio in the last page of my student exam book. I pasted a blank sheet of paper over it so it would not be visible.

And so I went to take my exam. And my grade: a perfect 30. [Tr.: Italian universities grade exams based on a scale from 1-30, 30 being the highest.] The first thing I did was immediately go to the station and catch the first train to San Giovanni Rotondo so I could give Padre the good news. Once I arrived at the friary, I rushed to the sitting room where Padre usually sat with some friends and other friars after the evening service.

As soon as he saw me and before I said anything, he said with a smirk, "So there's the face of someone who just got a thirty…I would have given you a thirty -- thirty kicks in the rear end! And you know what I think? That you take me for a deaf person. I told you to send me your angel just once, not five times. Take the photo out of your exam book, you're using a trick to take your exams."

As I did not have the book with me, I stood there clearly speechless. However, by now I was starting to get used to such outward manifestations of divine power that directed Padre's life. Thus, somewhere between happiness and amazement I approached him, knelt down, and with his usual sweetness he allowed me to kiss his hand. Spontaneously I said almost in a whisper, "Thank you Father." And he responded, "You just worry about studying, leave the rest to God."

> "I told you to send me your angel just once, not five times."
> --Padre Pio

So how is it possible on a human level to explain this event? How is it that Padre already knew everything before I even said a word? What was the common thread that linked that friar to the divine energy that does all things through the Holy Spirit? It was a great mystery that led me to some considerations.

I realized that people possess all the spiritual treasures they need to live a life full of success and happiness. One just has to be fully convinced that we are, first of all, spiritual beings; our spiritual nature sets in motion the divine power that is already within us. It is a divine power which is Peace, Love, Harmony and Wisdom.

We create what happens to us through the application of universal laws. Some laws help us obtain what we desire, the main one being that of faith.

We've all heard many times the expression, "have faith." Faith is the recognition of the invisible divine Spirit that embraces the universe and must be accepted with trust. When we have faith in ourselves and in God, we know that we are safe, loved and never alone. We must believe in our spiritual nature and be convinced that all things are possible through faith. We must have faith and trust in the divine light that is in our soul. We must believe to have faith, because it is faith that brings us to the Heart of God. And this is precisely what happened in the episode of the exam.

I had already noted that Padre Pio was an enlightened spiritual being -- a daily expression of Divinity who works through us. But in Padre Pio there was little humanity left; he was all spiritual, and this nature of his made him cancel out the five senses and the limited laws of human nature. But how is divine power set in motion? With faith!

In sending my guardian angel to him no less than five times, I had placed total trust in Padre Pio -- though perhaps lacking on the human plane. This act of faith in Padre Pio, an intercessor before the Most High, set in motion the law of cause and effect with the results we saw. Because everything starts with an act of faith that has nothing to do with reason: the one cancels the other out. The Gospel says it all, "Let it be done for you according to your faith" [Matt 9:29] and "Everything is possible to one who has faith." [Mark 9:23].

Padre Pio himself once said to his confessor that things happened naturally and not even he could give an explanation of the supernatural events surrounding his life. He used to say, "I pray and nothing else; it is God who works the rest." In fact, in Padre Pio there was no logical or human explanation for such events: mind-reading, telepathy, reading souls, description of events that had yet to occur or that would occur far away. This was all normal for those who could say like St. Paul, "It is no longer I who I live, but God who lives in me" [Galatians 2:20].

All the manifestations which divine power worked through him found their highest expression in the humility with which he presented the events by almost making light of them. For example, when he joked, "I would give you thirty kicks in the rear end," he acted like he had forgotten the extraordinary nature of the episode which had nothing human in it.

One evening, while he was returning to his cell, Padre Pio came across a childhood friend of his. He was visibly moved. I was present (behind Padre Pio), and Dr. Frisotti was at my side. This is one of the most beautiful images of the face of Padre Pio.

VISITING PIETRELCINA AND MARRIAGE!

It was February, 1966 and Father Lino Barbato was Minister of the Third Order of St. Francis [Tr.: now called the Secular Franciscan Order]. As such, he had to go to Pietrelcina to conduct some meetings and he asked me to accompany him. I did not want to turn down his invitation, as, among other things, I wanted to get to know the area where Padre was born and grew up. [Tr.: Pietrelcina is in the vicinity of Benevento on the opposite side of the Italian peninsula, about 170 km. {105 miles} from San Giovanni Rotondo.]

We stayed in Pietrelcina -- full of memories of Padre -- for about four days. I brought my camera with me and took advantage of my time there to shoot a home movie of the places most special to him which I had planned to show him as a gift. And so I did.

On the way back, in Foggia, I worked it out with Father Lino and the superior of the friary to show the home movie in Padre's cell. We even mounted the projection screen on his bed.

Padre Pio watched the entire movie with profound emotion. When he saw the church of Santa Anna where he was baptized, his voice broke with tears and he said, "Here is where I became a Christian." Then, turning toward me, he said, still moved, "My son, I am grateful to you. You have given me seventy-nine years of life. My gratitude is eternal, I will help you and I will assist you until the last moment of your life."

At these words, Father Lino interjected saying, "But Father, Adolfo would like to be 'compensated' for this work." But Padre responded, "What he gave me today is priceless." Then Father Lino said again, "Father, Adolfo would like you to preside over his wedding." At those words, Padre Pio's face became serious and after a moment, he added, "But he knows well that due to my physical condition

41

today I can no longer do such ceremonies." But then after a moment of silence, he continued, "Okay, so it shall be. It will be the last wedding of my life. And let it be on the 23rd." (It was a strange coincidence for us, but certainly not for him, as the 23rd was the date of his death).

Then he turned to me and said, "My son, remember that if priesthood is a mission, marriage is doubly so: sometimes, one of the spouses should be quiet, and other times the other one should." Then we said goodbye, and I returned to Foggia brimming with joy and excited to give Franca the good news.

> "In marriage...one of the spouses should be quiet, and other times the other one should."
> --Padre Pio

By then it was already toward the end of February, and I had the gall to say to my soon-to-be wife, "Franca, I have great news: Padre Pio is going to marry us on April 23!" I said April out of haste. She, however, was less than enthusiastic, "Have you gone crazy? How can we possibly prepare everything in such a short time?" Yet, after seeing my resistance, she gave in.

In his sitting room during a moment of affectionate dialogue.

In a few days we started to begin preparing the invitations. So, I called Father Carmelo to confirm both the date and the time. His response, however was, "But Adolfo, Padre Pio probably said he would celebrate your wedding in a moment of gratitude. But, you know well that due to his physical condition he can no longer handle such hardships."

But I persisted, "Father Carmelo, please at least grant me the courtesy of asking Padre directly. If he says no, I will surrender to the will of God." And so the superior obliged me and went to Padre Pio. After asking him to confirm, Padre Pio responded, "I said yes, and yes it will be. In fact, earlier I said I would celebrate in the small church, now, however, out of obedience I agree to celebrate in the large church and with full honors." Initially, Padre Pio wanted to celebrate in the small church which was very dear to him, yet the Superior insisted on the large church, expecting a large turnout of guests.

APRIL 23, 1966: MARRIAGE

And finally, the big day arrived. I was already in San Giovanni Rotondo a good half hour before schedule. I went straight into the sacristy to wait for Padre to come down so I could greet him before the wedding.

My siblings were with me along with the two witnesses, Mario Frisotti and Father Lino Barbato, in addition to the Superior, Father Carmelo, as well as Br. Giovanni and other friars including especially Father Pellegrino. [Tr.: Italian weddings do not use bridal parties; instead, as per canon law, they have two witnesses.]

Padre Pio in the sacristy preparing to celebrate my wedding.

As soon as I saw Padre Pio, my heart leapt with joy. He approached me with that heavy walk of his, and the light that emanated from his face was intense beyond all words. Only the eyes of the spirit could resist and appreciate that divine radiation. It seemed that his battered and bloody body was surrounded by a golden halo that radiated a strong white light.

I felt so much joy that my heart seemed to unite with his. Believe me, even today after so many years it is hard to explain exactly what I felt. I can only say that in that moment I felt at one with him, and inside me there was an explosion of infinite love. Once again I was able to see how his gratitude toward me and fatherly love made me overflow with joy.

Then preparations for the ceremony began. At a certain point, Padre said to Father Pellegrino, "Bring me the most beautiful stole." Indeed, they brought him a stole embroidered in gold given to him by a prayer group from New York. Then, turning to Prof. Frisotti and my brother, Saverio, he added, "Given how I felt, I should not have celebrated this marriage. Yet, I'm doing it because God commanded me to do it." He pronounced the words with regal solemnity.

And then the ceremony began. It would be pointless to speak of my emotion in seeing the image of God reflected in his face before me. His eyes, full of infinite love, conveyed this message to my heart, "My presence and my blessing hand will always be near you, hour by hour, step by step, especially in the difficult times of your life."

After the ceremony, I left my bride at the altar and accompanied Padre into the sacristy to say goodbye to him. Several days earlier, I had asked the restaurant, Santa Maria delle Grazie, to provide the same menu to the friars which I had arranged for the guests at the wedding banquet. But I had not told anyone, not even the superior. Yet, as soon as I arrived in the sacristy, after expressing best wishes to me again, Padre said to me to the amazement of all, "My son, why did you go through such trouble? The friars here are treated well and they lack nothing." [Tr.: It is not uncommon in Southern Italy to serve long, multi-course meals at wedding receptions.]

Yet another mystery with no explanation!

46

A copy of the document of matrimony.

Padre Pio sets out to celebrate my marriage (April 23, 1966)

Padre Pio performs our marriage, the past one he officiates
before he dies (April 23, 1966)

We're all there for the celebration of my wedding (April 23, 1966)

"I am celebrating this wedding because God commanded me to do it," said Padre Pio. HIs happiness radiated from his face, full of light.

49

An image of pleasure during the ceremony (April 23, 1966)

How much joy in his eyes!

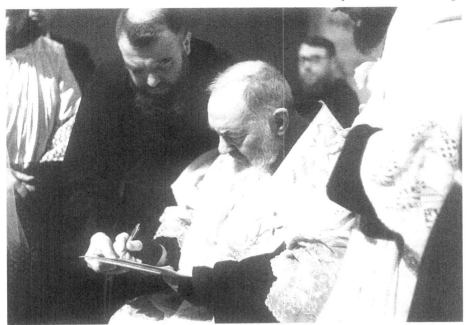

The solemn moment of celebration.

A moment during my wedding. The witnesses,
Father Lino Barbati (in the middle) and Dr. Frisotti.

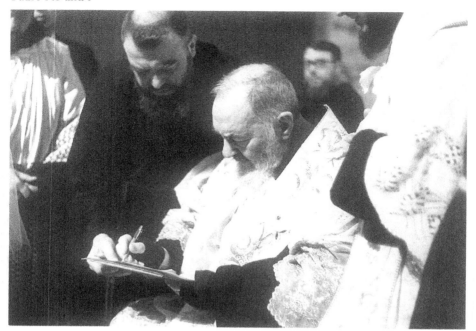

He signs the registrar of our marriage (April 23, 1966)

Another moment during the wedding.

Another image of Padre's happiness on April 23, 1966.

At the end of the celebration he said, "So, now I must say goodbye to you.
I bless you and be happy."

Padre Pio and I

HONEYMOON

The wedding feast was long and intensive, typical of the culture in Southern Italy. Yet, it also has its positive aspects such as, for example, having family members and friends all gather around the bride and groom to share in their joy at the beginning of a new life that will lead them to become one flesh before God, in "reciprocal comprehension," as Padre Pio used to refer to the sacrament of Matrimony.

But the surprise was to come in the late afternoon when Franca went into the bedroom to get changed for the trip. To her astonishment, she could not find her suitcase which she had prepared to bring on our honeymoon. I'll let the reader imagine the despair and panic we felt in that moment. So she retraced her steps and realized that out of haste, she had left her suitcase on the sidewalk by the door to the apartment.

We immediately called a neighbor and pleaded for her to take a look down by the door to see if the suitcase was still there by chance. After a few minutes, she called back and said that the suitcase was indeed still there. Thus, Padre Pio already worked his first miracle for us as a married couple! I have no other way of explaining how no one touched her precious suitcase after seven hours.

And so we began our journey north to Loreto. [Tr.: The city of Loreto, on the Adriatic Sea, is about 320 km. {200 miles} north of San Giovanni Rotondo; it is a popular pilgrimage destination site as it conserves the Holy House of Mary.]

SIRMIONE DEL GARDA

In a restaurant in Loreto, we met a couple from Pescara named Ivana and Emilio Giansante and took a liking to them immediately. [Tr.: Pescara, also on the Adriatic Sea, is about halfway between Loreto and Foggia.] They invited us to continue our journey north in their car, and so we did.

It was a Sunday afternoon when suddenly the interior of the car was filled with an intense aroma of rose and lily-of-the-valley. I knew the meaning of that fragrance right away and that it was a typical sign of the presence of Padre Pio among us. I felt a shiver run down my spine, and my heart lept with great joy. I instinctively felt the need to turn on the radio.

Precisely in that moment, the voice of Silvio Giglio [Tr.: a popular Italian radio broadcaster in the 1960s] was on the radio saying, "Dear radio listeners, today we are linked with San Giovanni Rotondo where you will be able to hear the voice of Padre Pio." After a few moments, the deep and raucous voice of Padre came on the air saying, "My Beloved children, especially those of you who are far away, I wholeheartedly send my blessing to you and to your families. Do not forget that suffering brings us closer to the Heart of God." I was so moved at that moment that I began to weep.

When I returned home, the first thing I did was go visit Padre to bring him a souvenir from the trip. I went into the sitting room next to his cell where Carlo Campanini was seated next to him in absolute silence. Padre Pio had a rosary in his hand and was deeply engrossed in what he called his "daily colloquies" with the Virgin Mary.

I knelt down and handed him my humble gift, saying, "Father, in Sirmione Del Garda …" But he did not let me finish my sentence and responded, "Did you really think I would leave you alone even for a moment?" [Tr.: Sirmione Del

Garda is a popular resort city on Lake Garda in Northern Italy.]

The phrase he had communicated to me a short time earlier, "I will help you and I will assist you until the last moment of your life," was already expressing itself concretely. Those words articulated with such sweetness -- a sweetness only a Father can offer -- caused me to feel a love for Padre I had never before experienced. I felt in my heart all the greatness of his Spirit. I wanted to embrace him, but out of modesty did not. I sensed again a strong emotion, as if our hearts were united in the name of the divine love that filled him. It was a love that is the essence of life itself -- a love that found a perfect interpreter in Padre who was ready to give it to anyone who came to him asking for help and comfort.

I realized in that circumstance that love is supreme and without love we are nothing. In this earthly journey of ours, we have a duty, a sacred duty, to love one another, to forgive one another and to serve one another. This is the direct line that brings us to the Heart of God.

Padre Pio lived a completely spiritual life. Other than the crucified body he dragged along so stoically, there was very little left of his humanness. His heart was full of light and divine energy, which you could feel when you were close to him without him even saying a word.

Oh, the joy I felt! He did not need his five senses any longer. He spoke as if his every word, his every gesture, was inspired by love, by the divine omniscience and omnipotence that had taken over his life.

I felt similar feelings of love a few years after his death. One night, in a moment of discouragement, I said to myself, "Father, have you forgotten me?" And sure enough, after a few days, I very clearly heard his voice tell me early one morning, "My son, I am with you more than you can imagine, together with your loved ones, with those who loved you, and with those whom you have loved. You are helped in everything that is possible. Have faith and pray, pray. I will always be by your side to help and encourage you."

I realized once again how important it was to thank God for having allowed me to know Padre Pio and to be his unworthy spiritual son. I also realized how important it was for me to honor that status and the many burdens it would entail.

I understood again how important it was to ask things from God in complete humility, and how it was even more important to be grateful when receiving.

But above all I was able to see that we must have faith -- the only therapy against constant worries and concerns. The more we thank God for what He gives us, the more we open our hearts to other blessings. He wants nothing more. If we open our hearts and minds to receive His blessing in the certainty that a Father will not deny a child, we will have fulfilled our nature as children of God.

THE BIRTH OF PIO

A few months after our wedding, we received the first good news: Franca was pregnant. The first thing I did was race to San Giovanni Rotondo to tell Padre. The first person I encountered was the Superior, Father Carmelo, to whom I joyfully communicated the forthcoming happy event. Father Carmelo said, "Thank you for what you have told me, but maybe you should let Padre Pio know yourself." So we went together into the parlor, where he was totally absorbed in his usual prayer.

This was the conversation we had:

Father Carmelo, "Father, Adolfo is here and he wants to tell you something."

Me, "Father, I wanted to tell you that I'm expecting a child."

Padre Pio, "You? You mean your wife…"

Me, "Yes, Father."

Padre Pio, "What do you want? A boy or a girl?"

Me, "Father, either is fine with me, as long as it's healthy. But I would be happy if it were a boy because I would like to give him two names, Francesco and Pio." [Tr.: Francesco was Padre Pio's baptismal name.]

Then a period of absolute silence followed… moments that seemed like they would never pass. An emotional intensity could be felt in the air. It seemed that something was about to happen, but no one knew what. We saw Padre Pio hold a handkerchief in front of his eyes as if to separate himself from his surroundings. It was obvious that he was talking to someone we could not see nor hear. Eventually we realized that in that moment he was offering himself as a sacrificial lamb for the new life that was coming into the world.

He then removed the handkerchief and revealed two tear-filled eyes emanating light. Then, he spoke again, this time in a trembling voice, "And thus it shall be:

your child will be born, will die, will live, and will be a boy."

His words were terrible; they left me breathless. I had no explanation. Like all things related to Padre Pio, this too, was a mystery.

Once I was back in Foggia, I gave Franca the news saying only that it would be a boy. I did not tell her anything else he said as I did not want to upset her.

Franca responded to my good news saying, "But do you really have to bother Padre Pio even for these things? I know you love him dearly, but you could have done without."

So on March 12, 1967, about twenty days before her due date, Franca went into labor. We immediately called the midwife, Lucia Trifiletti, who said we should call the doctor since the delivery was presenting apparent difficulties. So I hurried to call the gynecologist, Dr. Lo Conte.

Mysteriously, however -- I would call it Providence -- I happened to run into him at our very doorstep. He hurried upstairs to our apartment and indeed recognized complications in the delivery. He then applied his forceps and delivered a huge 5.8-kilogram baby [12.8 lbs.]. The baby was completely black and wasn't breathing. [Tr.: In that era, babies were born in the home with the assistance of a midwife; if there were complications, the mother was taken to the hospital or a doctor was called.]

The first thing the doctor said was, "Never mind the baby, there's nothing that can be done for it. Instead, we'll try to save the mother." So I took the baby and set him on the crib in the bedroom and rushed to the phone to call the friary of San Giovanni Rotondo.

I had them connect me to the superior and said, "Father Carmelo, our baby was born, but he's having great difficulty breathing. Please tell Padre." He replied that Padre Pio had had a high fever since the night before and could not be disturbed. After I begged him, he relented and went into Padre's cell. As soon as he arrived, when Padre learned I was on the phone, he said with great serenity, "Tell Adolfo not to worry, the child is in my hands." I took heart in his words.

> "Tell Adolfo not to worry, the child is in my hands."
> --Padre Pio

So for one week, my sister-in-law, Rina, and I took turns sitting with Pio to give him oxygen to help him breathe. His faint heartbeats slowly became regular.

The sacrifice was consumed and the miracle was completed: a child destined to die had come back to life. What seemed impossible had become possible thanks to the intercession of a stigmatized friar who bore the marks of God's only begotten Son who died to redeem all humanity on His body. Now everything was clear, "He will be born, will die, and will live." Everything had gone as planned, everything was as predicted seven months earlier.

The omniscient and omnipresent Holy Spirit illuminated the entire life of Padre Pio with His light. He acted in his daily life through his words, his works, and his miracles (as in the case of my son, Pio).

It is God who accomplishes everything, but he makes use of His cherished creatures like Padre Pio. With a man like Padre Pio -- who lived constantly filled with the light of the Holy Spirit, a sign of the divine Presence in him -- anything becomes possible. What may seem miraculous for us people was perfectly normal in the Spirit for Padre Pio. He was both creature and creator at the same time, having become a channel through which all God's omnipotence flowed, the infinite love of a tender Father who cares for His children more than we can imagine.

This is the silent reflection that I took away after the miraculous birth of Francesco Pio: The great truth of human life lies in becoming aware of the close connection of our lives with the life of God -- by opening ourselves completely to His infinite Love, by living in harmony with all that surrounds us and striving to be worthy and deserving of His attention. When we understand this, we have understood the fundamental truth of human life and it is then that we will witness extraordinary and miraculous episodes -- such as the birth of Pio -- as natural events.

A week after Pio's birth, I asked the Capuchin Provincial Minister, Father Giacinto, to celebrate a Mass of thanksgiving in San Giovanni Rotondo at the altar of St. Francis. He granted me my wish, and after the celebration we went to Padre's cell together, where I witnessed something very moving. Padre Pio refused to allow the Provincial to kiss his hand first saying, "You are my superior." Then Father Giacinto said to Padre, "Father, Adolfo is here. He wants to thank you…"

Padre Pio interrupted him and said, "You don't have to tell me, I alone know what I did to snatch that child from death." Everyone was speechless; it was the seal of a miracle. Then he added, "After so much effort, at least bring him here to me so I can see him." And so I did after a few months.

When I went in to his room, I brought my son to the wicker chair where Padre was absorbed in prayer as he wanted to caress him. Padre Pio blessed him and said, "[He will be] good, holy, and [live to be] very old. This child will be a giant in his life."

So much responsibility on little Pio.

A small gift to Padre.

FATHER, HAVE YOU EVER SEEN JESUS?

When I began going to Padre Pio, I was not yet twenty years old. Therefore, partly due to my age and partly to my impudent personality, I allowed myself a certain amount of license with Padre. Looking back today -- with a more serene mind and maturity that comes only with age and the awareness of who Padre Pio really was -- I would not dream of repeating [some of the things I said].

I'm saying this because one night, during one of those beautiful moments in which we were delighting in his presence, another friar asked him why he spoke so little. And Padre responded, "Because I have to be busy speaking with God." Indeed, he spoke with God constantly and unceasingly in prayer. He even recited fifty entire rosaries a day. He was so focused in his incessant and constant dialogue that he truly had little time left.

I was so enraptured by that heavenly face that radiated so much light I then asked him my question, "Father have you ever seen Jesus?" He stared at me, as if to say, "But how could such a question come to your mind?" Instead, he paused for a moment, and replied, "God is light. The more a soul is pure, the more it feels the splendor of that light." Then, after pausing for another long silence, he added, "And now no more questions."

I noticed right away that he did not respond, "Jesus is Light." Instead, he said "God is Light" to highlight that after his Ascension to heaven, Jesus and the Father were one, the Second Person of the Trinity was reunited with the First Person, the Father.

A few years later, I was in Rome where I bought a book by Emilio Crispo who died at the young age of twenty-nine. Entitled, *Un Diario di un Angelo* ("*Diary of an Angel*") the book is a diary of intimate colloquies written through the hands of his parents as he communicated to them from the afterlife. He says:

The concept of day or night does not exist here. There exists only light, which is different from earthly light because it emanates from the Spirit. The opposite is darkness, but it's not part of our world [i.e. the afterlife]. All this light is Vital Energy. The closer you get to Him (God), the more the light becomes intense, but it is not blinding. If it had a body, you could touch it, grasp it; in the center is God. The light vibrates, and in its pulse, it generates melodious music which becomes more harmonious and sweeter as you get closer to the divine source. (pg. 173) [Tr.: in the Italian edition]

Here, many years later, I had essentially received a confirmation of the answer Padre Pio had given me. And when I read this message, my heart leapt.

We are accustomed to thinking of that light as being far away from us and conceiving of God as something detached from us. However, this is not so. Instead, that divine light is within each one of us, as St. Paul reminds us [cf. 2 Cor 4:6]. We have a duty, inasmuch as we are children of God, to make contact with the divine source which is then the essence of our lives.

Unfortunately, however, this light has been buried by human nature and the negativity that comes with our humanity: selfishness, revenge, greed, resentment, fear, insecurity. Instead, we have the duty to replace this negativity with the positive thoughts of Peace, Love, Harmony, Serenity, Happiness, Forgiveness, and deep Faith.

We must look for the ray of light that is within us in order to go back to His source, the reason of our existence. Once this contact takes place, many things will be clearer. The clouds will dissipate, and we will see the world with another perspective.

Do you remember what Padre Pio said when he accepted me as a spiritual son? He said, "Be a worthy son, because the world is tired of words. It needs examples." In this is the profound and always relevant message of the word of Padre Pio.

We must discover within us the divine nature by living and honoring this heritage daily, especially as Padre used to say, "With silence, with prayer and with the continued application of the law of love." We must love everything and everyone, keeping in mind that it should be done according to our faith and that we will be judged by how we were able to love.

On the other hand, even within daily family life, all it takes is just a little misunderstanding to justify resentment which leads to no longer communicating. If only we could see the damage we cause to ourselves with these negative feelings, certainly we would think long and hard before falling into them. I insist on this, because such negativities take us away from that Light and make it dim, though it wants to shine in all its intensity.

Whenever a problem arises within the family or outside, we have the ability to resolve any situation through that spark of God that is always ready to intervene and help us bring balance back into our lives.

Let us never forget that the divine light is energy. "The energy of divine light is the center of all universal life."

THE MAN FROM FATIMA

It was a summer afternoon and the intense heat was oppressive -- typical of our region in Southern Italy. The only place where one could find the slightest bit of respite was in San Giovanni Rotondo with its decisively cooler temperatures. [Tr.: San Giovanni Rotondo has an elevation of 565 m. (1,854 ft.) while Foggia is at 76 m. (250 ft.).] So I went into the church in San Giovanni Rotondo to pray during the early hours of the afternoon. While absorbed in praying the Rosary, I was approached by an American man who asked me, "Where do I find Padre Pio?"

I responded to him, "He's upstairs in the friary, but he'll be coming down soon for Evening Prayer." Then I added, "If you stay here, you can come with me and I'll introduce you to him." He replied, "I am coming from Fatima, and I am asking Our Lady for grace for my daughter. She is very sick in America." I felt compassion and I told him, "Don't worry, when you meet Padre Pio, he will ask for a blessing for your daughter." About half an hour later, we went upstairs to wait for Padre to come out of his cell.

The wait seemed endless. My American friend was nervously pacing back and forth and was clearly quite distressed emotionally. I couldn't blame him. So I just prayed quietly and continuously in preparation to be worthy to meet Padre Pio.

At a certain point, the door opened and Padre Pio emerged more radiant than ever. In that instant, I was struck by his splendor and I was reminded of the words of the Gospel of Luke describing the transfiguration of Jesus: "While he was praying his face changed in appearance and his clothing became dazzling white ... And Peter said to Jesus, 'Master, it is good that we are here; let us make three tents, one for you, one for Moses, and one for Elijah.' But he did not know what he was saying. While he was still speaking, a cloud came and cast a shadow over them... Then from the cloud came a voice that said, 'This is my chosen Son; listen to him'" [Luke 9:29, 33-35].

For a moment, I had the distinct feeling that I was standing by Peter's side watching the transfiguration unfold. However, in the place of Jesus was Padre Pio -- a worthy and stigmatized representative of the crucified Christ on whom our heavenly Father bestowed all the divine gifts that can be granted to a beloved son.

So I went to him and said, "Father, this American gentleman would like a blessing for his sick daughter..." I didn't even finish my sentence before he interrupted me saying, "I know, Our Lady of Fatima already told me everything." I was speechless. Even

> "I know, Our Lady of Fatima already told me everything." I was speechless.

today after many years I still get goose bumps when I think of that incident.

My new American friend came over crying. He knelt down and begged Padre to pray for his daughter. Padre Pio shared in the pain of that father and said, "I will pray. But you pray, too." Then my friend, still weeping, took a fistful of dollars out of his pocket and attempted to give the money to Padre. Padre Pio, however, immediately became serious and said, "What are you doing with this money? If you want to make an offering, do so in the church. But most of all remember to pray." (It was as if he were saying that miracles cannot be bought with money, but only achieved through prayer).

My American friend, still in disbelief, turned to me and said, "How this is possible? You informed Padre Pio before with telephone?" The poor fellow hadn't understood a thing. Yes, Padre Pio had been informed, but by an extremely powerful phone -- that of the Holy Spirit -- the same who had spoken in the cloud during the transfiguration.

I have two possible explanations for this event. The first is that Padre Pio had availed himself of the gift of bi-location, one of many gifts granted to him by the Lord. In this case, while my friend was praying at Fatima, Padre Pio may have also been present there before the heavenly Mother to whom he felt a particular devotion to the point of even calling her *Mammina Mia* [my little Momma]. There are numerous cases of this throughout the history of the Church. For example, there is the levitation of St. Ignatius of Loyola and Santa Maria Maddalena de' Pazzi who would remain suspended in the air for long

70

periods of time. We can also recall the example of Mary of Agreda († 1665), the Servant of God who recorded around five hundred bilocations preceding the arrival of Franciscan missionaries in Mexico. When she prayed, she would go into ecstasy and become weightless; consequently, her body manifested phenomena that science could not explain.

Or the other possible explanation is that of prophecy, another gift which Padre Pio had. Here, a medieval axiom is perennially relevant, "If you want to experience God, first turn to the depth of your spirit." This refers to centers of vital energy within people that can be activated to awaken the hidden potential endowed to us by the Creator.

We can understand these statements more easily if we consider the witness of the saints, through which, thanks to their highly spiritual life, sacrifices, and prayers, these phenomena occur spontaneously. Even Padre Pio said to his confessor, "Not even I know how they take place; they are a mystery even to me." Clearly, there was no explanation in terms of reason, but there was from a spiritual perspective. Padre performed everything through the omniscience of the Holy Spirit, who -- by acting in the minds of the Saints, in this case Padre Pio -- gives rise to events we call miracles.

In Byzantine iconography, the gift of prophecy is represented by a beam of light placed in the icon at the center of the saint's forehead. In the history of the Church, there is the well-known example of the life of Blessed Anna Maria Taigi († 1837) -- a married woman from Rome and mother of seven children. From 1790-1791, while rapt in prayer, a bright light like the sun came to her and remained suspended over her forehead. She could gaze on it day or night by only lifting her eyes upward. Jesus Himself told her it was like a mirror in which she could see good and evil. Indeed for about fifty years, Blessed Taigi put her gift of prophecy at the service of all people, including even cardinals and the Pope. So we should not be surprised if Padre Pio also had the gift of prophecy together with the many gifts he received allowing him to be in constant contact with the mind of God.

This is another way we can explain certain phrases, statements or actions of his, such as calling someone by name whom he had never before seen, experiencing premonitions which then occurred, or when he called people or, when appropriate, drove off hardened sinners. These events initially seemed strange to those who were present to say the least. But over time, we became accustomed to them and took part in them almost unconsciously. We were so immersed in this sacred and surreal environment that we weren't even completely aware of all that was happening.

THE UNDERSECRETARY

One day I was given the task of accompanying a politician to Padre Pio -- an undersecretary who felt he needed to meet with Padre. [Tr.: In the US, this would be a high-ranking government official serving under a department secretary.] We met in the morning at Hotel Cicolella [in Foggia] and had breakfast together. He told me how he wanted to get to know Padre Pio and to place himself under his direction. He said that there had been three circumstances in his life in which he had made a vow, but then, for one reason or another, he had not been able to keep his commitments.

I reassured him and told him not to worry but rather to rely on the mercy of God through whom all things were possible. After all, how can a Father not forgive a son? We only have to re-read those beautiful pages of the Gospel that recount the story of the Prodigal Son [cf. Luke 15:11-32]. There is no way to describe the joy the Father feels when embracing a son who returns to Him. In fact, one day I asked Padre Pio, "Father, does God forgive everything?" Padre responded, "As a loving Father, God forgives all sins. But there is one sin that he forgives only with much effort: the ingratitude of man."

So that afternoon we set out for San Giovanni Rotondo. Once we arrived at the friary, we went upstairs right away to wait for Padre to come out of his cell. When I saw him, I customarily went forward, knelt down and kissed his hand which he allowed me to do with his usual sweetness. And every time I did so, I was always afraid of hurting him because I knew the pain he felt in those crucified hands of his. So I touched them lightly as if holding a butterfly in my hands.

I said right away, "Father, the undersecretary is with me and he would like your blessing." He responded, "Nice stuff you brought me here. Tell him that he made a vow three times and three times he failed." This was the last chance God was giving him.

I was shocked.

The politician did not even have the courage to approach him to kiss his hand, which also would have been difficult for the fact that Padre Pio kept walking without even deigning to look at him.

And here we see the other side of Padre Pio: the friar who was harsh and stern toward those who broke the law of God and neglected their duties as a Christian. And Padre, with his spiritual sensitivity, suffered enormously when confronted with such manifestations of ingratitude. His suffering increased in the wake of his task of bringing redeemed souls to the Most High with the help of the Immaculate Heart of Mary.

Never before were the prayers that the Virgin Mary taught Lucia at Fatima more relevant: "Most Holy Trinity, Father, Son and Holy Spirit I adore You profoundly and I offer you the most precious Body, Blood, Soul and Divinity of Jesus Christ present in all the tabernacles of the earth, in reparation for the outrages, sacrileges and indifference with which He Himself is offended."

Obviously, no one present had any way of knowing exactly what vows the politician had made and broken. Nor did we know what sins he was guilty of. Padre Pio, on the other hand, did, because, having the gift of reading souls, he could see what we could not. He used the most powerful radio of the Holy Spirit.

Clearly, through his universal Spiritual vision Padre Pio saw in this man all degenerate and perverse humanity who acted as if the human sacrifice of Christ had never happened. To them it was as if Christ had never come to earth to redeem humanity saying to all, "I am the Way, the Life, the Resurrection." It was also as if his sacrifice as a priest, which had been consuming itself since 1918, causing him unspeakable pain which stoically he kept to himself, had never happened either. All this caused him great pain.

But his suffering was increased even more during the act of consecration during the Holy Mass. In that moment, in which he held the Body and Blood of Jesus in his hands, he saw the violence done to the divine Heart caused by humanity with their sins. And his body, transfigured and becoming radiant as a blinding light, suffered, too. He suffered so much to the point of making him cry out groaning pain.

Humanity has lost the way of faith and no longer knows how to pray. Today, at the height of the technological era, we have everything we need and want. Yet, our hearts are arid, we lack the love of God, we no longer know how to smile, and we no longer know how to be happy. All this because we have forgotten that God within us continues to knock at our hearts. Only when we discover once again faith in God and in ourselves we will no longer be alone. Then, the things that are impossible today will become possible.

Things definitely went badly for my friend, the politician, that day.

TWO AMUSING EPISODES

Among the many stories that fill my mind, those I'm about to recount now come to my mind frequently because they were significant in my relationship of affection I had with Padre.

One afternoon, we were in the sitting room next to Padre's cell and, as usual, were enjoying his presence which bathed us in light and joy. It was nice to be at his side even if no one spoke. We realized we were privileged when we considered just how many people came from far and wide and couldn't even get near him. There were so many people suffering who would have done anything to have had the same privilege we did. We, however, had the good fortune of staying intimately in his presence, enjoying the magical atmosphere that was a gift to us.

At a certain point, Padre sneezed and could not find his handkerchief. So Father Lino said to me, "Adolfo, go into Padre's cell and get his handkerchief on the nightstand." I readily and joyfully went into his cell and took his handkerchief that was on the bedside table. I happened to notice some medals that Padre often gave to sick people, children, or whoever asked for them. I was tempted to take some, but decided against it thinking to myself, "You never know…"

I then returned to the sitting room and handed the handkerchief to Padre. However, he looked into my eyes and said, to the amazement of all, "Thank goodness you left everything as you found it, because I don't speak to *mariuli* [Tr.: dialect for thieves]."

Another evening I was in the small church with Mario Frisotti waiting for Padre to come down from the choir for the service of the Exposition of the Blessed Sacrament. The heat was stifling. We were seated to the left facing the altar. At a certain point, I said to Mario, "Let's go outside for a bit and get some fresh air, it's too hot in here." But Mario said, "No, let's wait and enjoy the old man a little more, we'll leave soon enough."

About half an hour later, Padre came down from the choir and went into the sacristy to get vested. Then the procession formed led by some altar boys and other friars with Padre Pio toward the rear. When he passed by us, he abruptly stopped and said, "Behold those who call other people old... as if they're young." Then he composed himself before proceeding regally toward his beloved Jesus at the altar where he prayed every evening the prayer of the Blessed Virgin by St. Alphonsus Liguori, his voice breaking with tears.

Padre Pio with Carlo Campanini and Father Lino Barbati

LAST CONFESSION

It was now 1968 and I was fortunate to have been able confess shortly before that fateful September 23 when Padre Pio was born to everlasting life. His would be a new life where there was no more suffering, but only glory after earthly Calvary and joy and happiness in the splendor of divine light. It would be a new life where, by his own admission, he would be able to do more and work better for all those who asked him to intercede before God.

I did not have an appointment in advance for confession that day, but the friar on duty recognized me and let me go in anyway. I never would have imagined that this was to be my last confession with him.

It is true that Padre was walking slowly and it was obvious that he was suffering more and more which he let others clearly see. But no one imagined that Padre was about to leave us. For us he was eternal, even in a physical sense. It was inconceivable to imagine Padre Pio dead.

At the end of confession, Padre said, "And what is your name?" I remained somewhat surprised by this question, which I thought might mean many things. But at that moment I had no explanation and so I said, "But Father, my name is Adolfo. I'm your spiritual son. Since my father died in 1962 you've been like a father to me." Surprising me once again he said, "My son, life is a gift that is not ours. It is given to us and is taken when God wants."

"Naked I came forth from my mother's womb, and naked shall I go back" [Job 1:21].

He paused for a moment, raised his right hand, placed it on my head and said, "*Arrivederci* [Until we see one another again] in heaven." Padre was saying goodbye to me for the last time.

At that moment, the passage in the Gospel of Luke describing the transfiguration came to my mind again. It was as if there was no longer a stigmatized and suffering friar in front of me who had heroically endured the marks of the crucifixion on his body for so many years. Instead, it was as if his face had become full of light, his body radiant.

I did not understand what he meant at that time. I thought he was having a "senior moment" due to his age, even if he often said how he could not wait to leave this earth and get to heaven. In fact, once Prof. De Caro asked him if he would be still with us for many years. But Padre responded, "And this is your wish for me? Do you do not see the condition I have been reduced to? I look forward to getting to heaven."

Indeed, on the morning of September 23, 1968 at about 4:00 AM, Prof. Frisotti and I both received the call. They told us that Padre Pio was dead. We immediately drove to San Giovanni Rotondo while I cried the entire trip. In that moment, the words Padre had told me during my last confession began to make sense.

When we arrived, he was still lying on his bed which had been placed in the middle of cell number 1. Thanks to the kindness of the Capuchin friars, I was allowed to stay close to his body, which was still warm, for a long time. I caressed his face and kissed his hands and feet. I stayed there in the friary with Prof. Frisotti for practically the entire day and did not return home until later in the evening. We returned to San Giovanni Rotondo for Padre's funeral.

Adolfo looking at the last confessional used by Padre Pio in 1968

MARIA GRAZIA PIA

By now it was 1971 and Padre Pio had been gone for about three years. It took some time, but eventually my initial feeling of loss subsided and I began to experience faith and serenity. Wherever I was, I felt him ever closer to me. In fact, this was confirmed through events and circumstances that occurred frequently. Those words he had said to me that day, "I will help you and I will assist you until the last moment of your life," kept running through my mind.

Of the many events that took place after his death, one that deserves special mention is the birth of Maria Grazia Pia. It was the beginning of May in 1971, early in the morning -- that time of day so dear to him when he celebrated Mass. I was still asleep when I suddenly felt his presence next to my bed. I heard his voice clearly say, "My son, have faith, pray, and be a worthy son. Soon we will go together to see Maria Grazia Pia who will be born on a beautiful day." I felt these words on my heart unspeakably and sweetly. It was as if Padre had spoken from within my heart.

I woke up suddenly and immediately said, "Thank you Father. If it is so, I will baptize her within twenty-four hours to help a soul in purgatory. And I will choose your niece, Pia Pennelli, to be her godmother."

And so it was. Maria Grazia was born on May 12, 1971, and I had her baptized the next day, a feast consecrated to Our Lady of Fatima, with Pia Pennelli standing as her godmother.

I must say that we had no way of knowing if it would be a boy or a girl. In that era, medicine was not what it is today and we didn't have modern technology capable of determining a baby's sex in advance like we do today. And plus my wife did not want to know anyway.

So when Franca went into labor on the morning of May 12, I drove speedily to the hospital of San Giovanni Rotondo arriving shortly before 8:00. As soon as we arrived in the obstetrics ward, I immediately went looking for Dr. Pavoni. When I found him, I said, "Doctor, please come quickly. Maria Grazia Pia is about to be born." Pavoni, with a playful smirk, said, "Okay, I know how much you love Padre Pio, but it seems a bit exaggerated to involve him in this right now. The important thing is that the child is born and that your wife has a good delivery."

Maria Grazia was born just after 8:00 AM. Shortly thereafter, Dr. Pavoni came up to me with the good news, saying, "You were quite right, you have a beautiful little girl." And when I explained the events preceding the birth of Maria Grazia, he was moved and added, "Indeed you have much faith. It's obvious that Padre truly loves you." So on the afternoon of May 13, we had refreshments with the Pennelli family and others.

This is just one of many episodes -- perhaps the most significant -- that took place after the death of Padre Pio. There are still others, and some are very moving. But they highlight the love that unites this great Saint and a great sinner like myself.

"When you call me, and come and pray to me, I will listen to you. When you look for me, you will find me. Yes, when you seek me with all your heart, I will let you find me -- oracle of the LORD -- and I will change your lot" [Jeremiah 29:12-14]. These beautiful words of the prophet Jeremiah encapsulate the meaning of my relationship with Padre.

TODAY AS YESTERDAY

My faith journey began when I met Padre Pio in July, 1953: seeking God through this beloved son of His, a worthy representative of the crucified Christ on earth. I have always seen Padre Pio as the highest form of expression of God in the twentieth century, a gift of God's great love for humanity.

For me, Padre Pio represented the key with which to directly access the Heart of God. By entrusting myself to him and abandoning myself to his tender fatherly love, he was always ready to take whatever I asked directly to God. And how could God not grant the requests of a son so dear to Him?

In a nutshell, Padre Pio powerfully entrusted all his prayers and requests to the Heart of God through the intercession of the Virgin Mary. And this is the secret of the vast numbers of miracles that occurred in the past and still occur today. When we entrust ourselves to her intercession for whatsoever our needs may be, when it is for our own good, we can be assured that we will always receive an answer.

Today as yesterday.

Because today, sanctified by the Church, Padre is the pure light of God. He is present within us through the Holy Spirit who is the sanctifying grace that responds to all our requests. The Holy Spirit is the Third Person of the Trinity: He is omnipotent, omnipresent, and omniscient. He is in us, and we are in Him. We must become channels through which all divine love flows. The light of the Holy Spirit illuminates our path and the omnipotence of the Holy Spirit guides us in everything.

It is God who accomplishes all the works, by using -- as in this case -- saints like Padre Pio. When we are filled with the light of the Holy Spirit, we can observe the great miracle which every person can witness. Our every effort will not fail, and our every wish will be granted.

But to achieve this, we must empty ourselves of our troubled human nature. A mind that is agitated or oriented toward human affairs is like putting a dam along a river preventing the water from flowing regularly. In other words, it prevents the grace of God from coming to us.

Instead, when the turmoil subsides and when our minds and our hearts are quieted, then our faith increases and the presence of God in us begins to manifest itself. It continually knocks on our hearts to give us life in abundance if only we let Him enter. Padre Pio was all this. He was completely emptied of his human nature to the point that he became, as St. Paul says, a "temple of the living God" [2 Col 6:16].

Certainly, it is not easy for anyone to undertake this journey. Yet, we must believe that we will never be asked to make sacrifices beyond our abilities. Our job is to honor the divine Presence within us wherever we are called to action: in our families, our communities, our workplaces. We should say to ourselves in every moment of the day, "I live, move and act in God who manifests himself within me at all times."

Padre Pio said to me over and over, "Be a worthy son." All of us, too, should say often, "Let us strive to be worthy sons of God." Our ultimate goal should always be to move from tension to calmness, from outer silence to inner peace, and from inner peace to contemplation of the God who lives within us. We must become aware of the presence of God within us.

And then finally, we will arrive at intimate union with God. This is the illumination which St. Teresa of Avila depicted as a mystical experience granted only to a few. Nor should we forget St. Anthony the Abbot (about whom St. Athanasius wrote) who "prayed almost always, because he learned that he had to pray silently and interiorly" to arrive at intimate union with God.

And what about Padre Pio? He, too, had fulfilled this. A man of prayer, he recited fifty entire rosaries a day. I don't recall ever seeing him without a rosary in his hands. This was his way of praying unceasingly to God and it demonstrates why he was surrounded by complete silence when he prayed. Because

> He recited fifty entire rosaries a day. I don't recall ever seeing him without a rosary in his hands.

in those moments he never separated from the rosary.

Every now and then he spoke to someone to say things that were profoundly meaningful. For example, he said to me once, "Be careful on your next exam, if you don't study hard, you'll fail." And in fact, that is precisely what happened. Another time, he said to a different spiritual son, "How is it that you don't realize you have a flat tire? Look, now you've made me become like a chauffeur."

One evening a brother friar said to Padre in dead silence, "Father, why do you never speak?" And he responded, "Of course I do, I pray and when I pray, I speak to God." Padre Pio's long silences were significant in that he was then focused on God. Moreover, silence is the language of God. In silence the doors of the presence of God open within us.

In the solitude of his cell, he spent his time in constant meditation. There he would find his inner self and there was his only peace. And in his inner peace, with his mind fixed on the suffering Christ, he went into ecstasy.

"Then you shall call, and the LORD will answer, you shall cry for help, and he will say: 'Here I am!'" (Isaiah 58:9). There is no better example than the words of St. Benedict -- who took inspiration from this passage of Isaiah in citing God's promise [in the Prologue of the Benedictine Rule] -- that refer to the deep spirituality of Padre Pio who was an instrument in the hands of God to convert sinners and help a suffering humanity.

POPE JOHN PAUL II

On May 24, 1987, my native city of Foggia was blessed by an apostolic visit of Pope John Paul II. Preparations were begun roughly one year earlier, and our archbishop (now a cardinal), Salvatore DeGiorgi, had asked me to lend a hand. So we began making trips up to Rome to prepare.

And finally, the big day arrived. My job was to authorize the press, provide accommodations, and organize the lunch to be held at the bishop's palace. At the time, I was serving as secretary of the M.G. Baron Foundation [Tr.: a non-profit rest home for the elderly in Foggia run by religious women]. Thus, I had the opportunity to use the nuns, as the [Vatican] Secretary of State had expressed a wish to avoid using non-local personnel.

It was my honor and pleasure to personally serve Pope John Paul II. Before lunch ended, the Pope invited me to sit between him and Dr. Buzzonetti, his personal physician. Archbishop DeGiorgi then said to the Pontiff, "Your Holiness, Mr. Affatato was a spiritual son of Padre Pio."

The Pontiff then turned to me and asked, "So you knew him well?"

"Of course, Holiness," I responded.

"Tell me something about Padre Pio," he requested. So I began to relate some stories that came to mind. After a pause, he said, "Continue speaking." After some more time passed, Fr. Stanislaw, his secretary, motioned to his watch, as the Holy Father's schedule was already tight. Then Archbishop DeGiorgi intervened and said, "Holiness, Mr. Affatato is a worthy collaborator of mine. In fact, this organization is all due to his merit."

The Holy Father then said promptly, "I am quite grateful for everything you have done for me."

And I said, "Holiness, make Padre Pio a saint very soon."

87

> "Did you know that I keep a collection of letters of Padre Pio on my night table next to my bed?"
> --Pope John Paul II to Adolfo

"If I had it my way, I would have already made him a saint," replied the Pope. "But you know that the Church takes her time. Nonetheless, we will try to speed things up. Did you know that I keep a collection of letters of Padre Pio on my night table next to my bed?"

He then blessed me and we said goodbye to one another. I saw Pope John Paul again that evening and the following morning during his visit to San Giovanni Rotondo when he prayed at the tomb of Padre Pio.

About a month after the Pontiff's visit to Foggia, I returned to Rome with Franca, my wife, and Archbishop DeGiorgi. There we were blessed to pray the Rosary together with the Holy Father in his personal chapel. Afterwards, they thanked me and I was given a medal with the image of the Pope which was coined in commemoration of his visit to Foggia. The Pope also personally gave me a rosary.

Several years later, in 1999, the beatification of Padre Pio took place, followed by his canonization in 2002. On both occasions, I had the great honor of being invited to sit in the platform reserved for the authorities. It was such a sight! I was so emotional at seeing so many people coming from all over the world! Padre Pio was right when he said, "I will make more noise from heaven than from earth." The Church knelt down before this beloved son of hers who made suffering and charity toward his brothers and sisters his rule of life. Indeed, the entire world witnessed this worthy son of St. Francis, who had made the redemption of souls his purpose of life.

All this was part of his spirituality, because Padre Pio concretely bore fruit -- through the accomplishment of the House for the Relief of Suffering -- which was the result of his prayers and of his crucifixion during life as he offered, in his words, "Relief in body and in soul to so many suffering people." How relevant are the words of St. James, "Faith is completed through works" [cf. James 2:22].

Cardinal DeGiorgi presents me to the Holy Father, John Paul II (May 24, 1987)

The Pope says to me, "Thank you for all you have done."

We set out toward the procession of vehicles that is already
waiting for us near the bishop's place.

Posing for the official photograph for the press.

The Pope gives me a rosary as a gift.

THE NECESSITY OF PRAYER

Never before has there been a crisis of morality and values such as today, as Pope Benedict XVI recently stated. Nor has the world ever needed prayers as much as now. Once again Padre Pio was a precursor as he invited all people to continuously pray and implore the mercy of God.

Mind you that Padre Pio's method of prayer was beyond merely reciting words. Words are useless unless accompanied by behavior as true children of God in which we place our minds and attitudes in sync with the universal law of harmony and love. How many people observe the precepts of the Church almost out of rote, all the while forgetting to renew their minds! Instead, how many make prayer, love and gratitude their way of life?

God decreed through his commandments for us to love Him with all our heart, with all our soul and with all our strength. This is the attitude that enables us to be able to live in the divine nature of Christ. In fact, Padre Pio often said, "Please, don't make me look bad" [Tr.: In other words, act as a worthy spiritual son.]

When we get away from this Christian attitude, God can become obscure in our minds and distant from us. There is the risk that He becomes the God of wrath and punishment. We know quite well, however, that this is not correct. Instead, the law of love allows us to focus on the true nature of God as a caring, gentle and affectionate Father who cares about the fate of His children.

When we learn Christ's message well, then we will realize that charity is one of the easiest commandments to follow. Then it is beautiful to love our neighbor as ourselves because all people will have become an inseparable part of the one God who burns in the hearts of all.

SUFFERING

As a worthy follower of St. Francis of Assisi, Padre Pio asked God for two gifts: to experience the same suffering as our Lord Jesus and for his heart to be filled with love for all humanity. These are the two pearls that made Padre Pio a giant in the Church and the first priest ever to bear the stigmata. [Tr.: Before receiving the stigmata on Mount Laverna, St. Francis asked the Lord for these same two gifts; Francis was a deacon, not a priest.]

I do not believe it is necessary to delve into the topic of suffering and Padre Pio here, as those before me have already done so and in great detail. Nonetheless, it could be said that Padre's motto was the following: pray, suffer, and offer. In this, I mean that he gave his consent to allow the love of God to flow completely through his life. And thanks to his heroic offering, any soul who turned to him was purified and spiritualized. By lowering himself into Christ's suffering, Padre Pio was able to work for the conversion, glorification, and sanctification of souls.

But the love of God the Father was stronger than Padre's sorrows, and few people ever fully understand the salvific power of suffering. By offering his pain, by merging his suffering with the Blood of the crucified Christ poured out like a river of purification and redemption, so many wondrous deeds took place and so many miracles still continue to occur.

Padre Pio did not spare himself for anyone; instead, he gave himself to all up to the limits of his strength. He constantly and passionately told everyone who approached him that Jesus and Mary desired to be loved through continuous prayer and a holy life. He had but one concern: to live in God at the service of all people. And, until the last day of his life, by offering himself as a victim in the name of humanity, he was faithful to his mission.

I would like to point out that there was not enough medicine in the entire world to treat all the ailments he had. Instead, his only solace was in prayer, the Eucharist, and in his continuous colloquies with God and the Virgin Mary which took place in the silence of his cell. Just consider for a moment how much he suffered as a walking crucified man for fifty years. How much he endured for love of God to whom he offered himself as a victim to ransom the souls of sinners and in reparation for the continual offenses of all mankind!

Yet, in addition to his physical sufferings, Padre Pio also had to endure others created from within his own Franciscan Order. Some of his fellow Capuchins in Rome were continually launching investigations culminating in the decision to transfer him elsewhere, which was averted only by a revolt by the faithful. Nonetheless, from 1931-1933 when he was prohibited from having any contact with the faithful, he accepted the orders that came from Rome with humility. But despite his isolation, what really made him suffer was not being able to hear confessions. Who knows if he ever asked himself how many souls he could not redeem and bring back to God during those years? Despite this turbulent period, however, he always remained serene and full of God's grace that shone forth from within.

LONG SILENCES

We are now arriving at the conclusion of what was supposed to be a simple publication of the diary of my relationship with Padre Pio. Instead, as the work progressed, I continued on and allowed myself to delve into various considerations that came to mind. So what do I have left to say after all these years since Padre Pio was reborn in heaven?

First of all, beyond the fact that the Church has now proclaimed Padre a saint, and therefore venerable, today, many years later, the Padre Pio I once knew has always remained the same. I still feel as if he is constantly close to me, and I cannot separate myself from him even for a moment. I still see him with his burdened step, hunched over beneath the weight of the cross of so many sins of humanity taken upon himself. I still see him with his deep voice and hear his enlightened words that entered my heart and have never left. It is as if everything Padre told me were written inside me in letters of fire. I can remember perfectly every episode, every moment, and every facial expression of his sweet face from which divine light emanated.

I remember his words, "I will help you and I will assist you until the last moment of your life" and "My hand is on you and on your aspirations day by day." These, along with many other phrases, run through my mind day after day and give me deep faith and certainty that he is always by my side as he has shown even after death.

Only those who knew Padre and were close to him can understand the emotion I still feel today when I reflect on these stories and write about them. They make my heart beat stronger.

He still says today, with divine omnipotence, "Behold, I am here today as yesterday." And I rejoice, I rejoice, so much in this with tremendous happiness within.

Padre Pio had certain qualities that have remained particularly etched in my mind. Let me begin with his long silences which are, in my opinion, one of the keys to understanding his supernatural nature.

When someone redirects their life from the exterior to the interior, on a spiritual level, the interior self -- the most profound part of the person -- takes the place of the ego. Then the divine self within takes command of their life. In the sanctuary of his soul, in silence and recollection, God spoke to Padre Pio directly to his heart.

For saints like Padre Pio, listening is not merely hearing with the ears, but participating in humanity's "pulse" in tandem with the Holy Spirit which illuminates thoughts before they are expressed with words. The sign of contact made with God is contemplation, and the sign of contemplation is silence and prayer.

During his long silences, punctuated only by the movement of his fingers on rosary beads, the spiritual delight was amazing. An energetic strength charged with heavenly presence within him emanated from his persona. I cannot express what I felt in those moments as every word is inadequate to describe the boundless joy that overflowed from my heart.

In involuntary witness with another Prelate from the Holy See.

> Punctuated only by the movement of his fingers on rosary beads, the spiritual delight was amazing.

During those times, my mind was emptied of every thought and concern. My body was calm and relaxed and I had complete control over my senses and feelings. I felt lightness and a joy that pervaded my entire self. I felt well, very well.

When you experience something like this -- involving all your emotions -- you never want it to end. Only those who have felt this know what I mean. Only those who had the good fortune to experience such events personally can have a more realistic picture of who Padre was than those who would write about him after just historical studies.

It goes without saying that while we meditate in profound silence, we speak with the Holy Spirit who is in us. And God always answers the prayers of His children. In silence, the mind is illuminated and the truth is revealed.

People are usually accustomed to relationships with others based only on the outward aspect. But they forget that the person is only the mask that covers one's true nature which we cannot see with our eyes. Behind this veil is the true being -- the soul, a deposit of the divine light -- present within everyone speaking to us through the Holy Spirit. And then it happens -- as if by a miracle -- that we are able to see with the eyes of God that which previously we could not see; we can hear that which we did not understand before; and we can accomplish that which previously seemed impossible to us.

People need to understand that they could solve all their existential problems by setting in motion the potential that is within their souls. That which the senses are unable to perceive is within the reach of intuition; its range is infinite. With this divine faculty, people can have access to direct knowledge of all things including their solution -- and not by just reason and experience, the limits of which are well known. Thus, it makes sense that when Padre was asked for an explanation of the miracles attributed to him, he responded, "It's a mystery also to me." In fact, there is no rational explanation for miracles.

Those like Padre Pio, who had a strong spiritual life, have well-developed intuitive capabilities. In Padre Pio's case, however, we are much further because we are dealing with supernatural phenomena such as reading hearts and thoughts in addition to prophecy. A medieval mystic, Albert the Great, once wrote, "Ascending to God is nothing other than moving inward. He who enters into himself, by penetrating the depths of his soul, goes beyond himself and truly arrives at God."

I have dwelt on this aspect at length here because it is one of the characteristics of Padre I recall with great pleasure. Padre Pio always retreated to the silence of his soul, he did not speak much, and he constantly prayed the Rosary. It was almost as if he were present among us in his body only symbolically while his mind was somewhere else connected with God.

In his meditative stillness, Padre Pio had the goal of conscious connection with the center of his life: God. When one reaches this goal through a life of terrible suffering, prayer, renunciation, and the conquest of souls, God could only respond by giving this beloved son of His the marks of the crucifixion.

When all is calm within, when every voice and clamor have ceased, then silence is reached. Then one can enter beyond the mysterious threshold. It is in silence where one finds the great source of life: divine light. It is a wonderful communion beyond human limits, because humanity is then immersed in the Divinity that dwells within. As the poet says, "Being shipwrecked in this sea is sweet to me" [Tr.: From Giacomo Leopardi's poem, *L'infinito* "The Infinite," written in 1819].

So how one can find a logical explanation for such things that happened in Padre Pio's life even though it all seems completely illogical? In silence, divine powers dormant in man are manifested. God is pure spirit. Padre Pio understood all this perfectly by becoming a worthy representative of divine omnipotence. I can personally testify that when he spoke there was little of humanity; instead, he was illuminated.

I recall one night in his sitting room with several other people. There was a man present who was insisting on recommending a sick woman to him. Padre Pio, instead, said to him, "Think instead of your own soul." I found out later that the man died one week later. Padre Pio was able to see the imminent death of that man who was speaking. And he responded by inviting him to prepare his own soul which was close to God's judgement.

Once again, in the words of Professor Medi, Padre represented the "naturalness of the supernatural."

THE LEGACY OF PADRE PIO

How blessed was that warm July day in 1953. That afternoon, a ray of the divine descended upon me and forever changed my life. After all these years, I cannot imagine how my life would have turned out today had that encounter never taken place.

I owe all that I am and all that I have achieved to the divine goodness used by this beloved son of Yours, Padre Pio, who guided me and still guides me from heaven. To you Padre Pio, I offer my gratitude because, as a steward of God's strength, I see how you worked in my life. And I acknowledge with gratitude and love everything you have poured out and continue to pour out on these little hands of mine.

The question I often ask myself is this: have I been a worthy spiritual son of Padre Pio? Have I done what he asked of me? Certainly, when I consider what I received, I should have given more. Yet, it is just as certain that I loved Padre with all my heart and made him a point of reference in my family as well as in my professional life: I've brought him into the hearts of countless people I have come in contact with, and I have brought many people to San Giovanni Rotondo placing them, according to his promise, under his blessing.

Unfortunately, however, my human nature has not allowed me to reach perfection as he would have liked. Yet, I trust greatly in the mercy of God and in His great paternal heart which makes all things possible.

Up until my encounter with Padre Pio, I had the same vision of life as most people and my worldview was limited by the bounds of reason: everything was centered on my ego and external personalities and I was oblivious to and ignorant of the spiritual journey of interior growth. Yet, when I crossed through the door that day, I could not turn back. And that door was Padre Pio.

My transformation had begun and I began to understand that I was made up of more than merely the structure of bones, skin and flesh that comprised my fleshly body. I then began to understand that the true self was invisible and intangible to the five senses which can only perceive form. Instead, I began to learn that the center of the human being was the soul. And precisely here is where the divine spark resides which created us and keeps us alive by the divine Spirit -- the tangible presence of God within.

I realized that the essential pathway to consider myself a new creation was to believe that I was not limited to my physical form. Everything the Spirit of God inspires within is received and realized in the form of thought which is then externalized in words and actions. As St. Paul says in the Letter to the Romans: "Do not conform yourselves to this age but be transformed by the renewal of your mind, that you may discern what is the will of God, what is good and pleasing and perfect" [Romans 12:2].

And this transformation takes place precisely in the present; in the here and now people realize that they can make a daily miracle of their lives. The first great miracle had taken place: I realized that Padre was not a human being who was having a spiritual experience; rather, he was a spiritual being who was having a human experience.

My ongoing talks with Padre Pio continued to convince me that our true self -- the soul -- cannot die, because the divine light that is within us is the same energy that sustains the entire universe. Therefore, we have no reason to fear death.

So what exactly did Padre Pio do for me? In essence, he did the same thing he had done with all those with whom he came into contact. He took my soul, turned it inside out like a sock, cleaned it up nicely, and presented it to the Lord as a new creation. In a nutshell, he removed the blindfold that prevented the light of God from shining and illuminating my earthly journey. The great soul-surgeon that he was, he removed all the scabs and scales of human misery I was carrying around.

I understood that behind every visible form exists a divine, omnipotent intelligence to support it; it is omnipresent, omniscient and invisible, but real nonetheless.

What I did not know before meeting Padre Pio -- and now I am convinced of this -- is that God lives within us with all His wisdom, His love, His intelligence and His omnipotence. He is there as a kind, caring, and affectionate Father toward His children and asks only to be loved in return. When we have demonstrated by our deeds that we love Him above all else, then He is ready to hear all our prayers that are supported by a deep faith, "To see what the human eye cannot see" and "To receive that which we believe in our hearts." This is my concept of the faith life.

But this is only the first aspect of what I learned from Padre Pio's spiritual direction. Another very important aspect was the new concept of life he taught me: life should be no longer considered as a "struggle," but rather a continual "self-conquest" and a slow return to the House of the Father. Here again I recall the words of St. John, "I came that they may have life and have it more abundantly" [John 10:10].

The moment I walked through that door, my life was completely transformed. And today, after all these years, I can see how the words of the Gospel are relevant and true. It is my hope that these memoirs of mine may be a testimony to the love of God that has been poured out on me through my spiritual father: Padre Pio.

I am still moved at how I received everything I asked for. It is as if an invisible hand opened all the doors and eliminated all the obstacles in my way. When Padre Pio told Father Carmelo of Sessano to accompany me to Naples to see Marquise Boschi and ask her to help me find a place to live, Padre strongly recommended for me to, "Study, because you will climb very high ladders." That was in 1957.

And today, after so many years, everything has come true. I went from being a modest accountant in a firm selling electrical equipment, to graduating from the university, passing the professional state exams and becoming a Registered Auditor. Yet, I never needed any of those titles professionally, because, in fact, my next job was at Telecom [Tr.: the state telephone company] where I worked as an official. Yet, I gave witness to my faith and left Telecom for the Maria Grazia Barone retirement home where Padre sent me, saying, "Go there. They really need you."

My choice led to some arguments with my wife, as I was on a promising career path as an official with Telecom. Instead, however, I gave up a promotion and job transfer in order to manage a simple retirement home. Yet, my decision was the result of an act of love for Padre Pio and trust in what he told me to do.

I stayed at the Barone Foundation for twenty years. I worked very hard and transformed it from an abandoned poorhouse to a modern home for the elderly with every amenity and comfort. Faith worked wonders.

Then, in 1989, I experienced my "great leap": I was appointed General Agent at INA-ASSITALIA, an Italian insurance agency, which also allowed me to pave the way for my son, Pio, to succeed me. From the time of my appointment, my business was a huge success. I continued to notice the presence of Padre Pio in my work including the fact that the Foggia branch is today considered the high point in my region [of Apulia], and was even recognized by the business magazine, *Il Mondo* ("The World"). The reward for my faith had arrived, and with it prosperity.

Once again the words of St. John are apropos here (which I use in reference to my own calling), "No one can come to me unless the Father who sent me calls him" [John 6:44]. How blessed was my calling by Padre Pio, "Adolfo, come here."

But why me? I've heard it said that you don't argue with a calling, you just respond to it. And from that day on, I placed myself under the spiritual guidance of Padre Pio.

I believed in and I surrendered myself into the arms of Padre. I allowed myself to be caressed by his crucified hands -- fount of miracles. Believe me, my faith was concrete, because I saw how everything I desired was eventually fulfilled.

Here, once again, I quote from St. John, "Whoever believes in me, as Scripture says: 'Rivers of living water will flow from within him'" [John 7:38]. The Gospel is not limited to Sunday Mass; instead, it is more relevant than ever, today as yesterday.

If people understood the testimonies left by the apostles and tried to live in harmony with the Word of God, they would see their lives change. No longer would they walk in darkness, but their earthly journey would be guided by the divine light that surrounds them with all God's love. We do not know where we could arrive because we do not know the potential of our minds. We have only one duty: to honor and give witness to the presence of God within us with our lives.

Saint Germain once wrote in his meditations, "Be still and know that I am God [Psalm 46:10]. Meditate deeply on these words in the total silence of your soul. I am the source, the origin of your life, of every joy and of every happiness."

When we have internalized the Christian message, we will abandon ourselves to the will of God and we will become aware that His divine love guides our lives. That light will shine in all His power, and nothing will be impossible, because nothing is impossible with God.

The important thing is that all our achievements and everything we have received be used altruistically. In other words, we must become a channel flowing abundantly with divine service to those who need it. In this, Padre Pio had become a dispenser of grace.

But the light within us is not the result of some magic formula or special calculations; instead, it is only the result of a life full of love, forgiveness, compassion, charity and infinite patience combined with a complete absence of rancor, hatred, resentment, revenge or greed. When we unite these positive sentiments to our prayer and the nourishment of the Eucharist, God expresses His love for us by giving us a transcendental vision of who we are and what we can achieve. Then we can say, "I am a child of God. Holy Spirit, guide my life and be master of my thoughts and feelings. Take possession of my activities and transform everything with your power."

When we have done all this, there is one last step to complete: pray the words in the Our Father -- "Thy will be done." Then the connection between the human mind and the divine mind will be accomplished. We will then have faith that whatever happens is always for our good, even though many times -- due to our human limitations -- we cannot see it.

Instead, we must overcome all this by firmly believing that God is a loving Father who only wants what is good for us. His way of reasoning is divine. He knows what we do not know, He sees what we do not see, and He knows if what we ask for is good and just for us.

"If everything is in God, it is equally true that God is in everything." Nothing can be outside of God. All people are contained within the divine mind in which we all live and move and exist.

When our lives are in harmony, we fulfill the knowledge of God. And when we have realized His presence within us -- and are fully conscious of it -- we will enter a sphere of light and love that is the true state called heaven. This was the state in which Padre Pio lived, always full of divine grace, supported by the aid and help of the heavenly Mother to whom he was much attached.

Everything was light in him; his every gesture and every word were illuminated by divine light. Padre Pio was no longer a human friar; he had become a living crucified Christ. The many miracles and extraordinary episodes attributed to him while he was still alive are proof of this.

I STILL HAVE MY STRENGTH

It was November, 1966 and it was so cold it seemed it would snow at any moment. Prof. Frisotti called me in the morning telling me that we needed to pick someone up from the train station who was coming from Rome to see Padre Pio that afternoon. However, the train was delayed, and we arrived late for Evening Prayer after Padre had already gone up to his cell.

So we went to the porter, Father Vincenzo, and we requested that he let us go up. Despite our insistence, however, his answer was a firm no. The only person who could help us was the Superior. Looking back, I can't blame Father Vincenzo, as he was only acting under obedience. So we kindly asked him to call Father Carmelo, which he did. We repeated our request and pointed out that the delay was not due to our negligence, but due to a train delay and the gentleman with us really wanted to talk to Padre. The Superior understood the situation, made an exception, and allowed us to go up.

Padre Pio was in his sitting room with a few close friends. When he saw us, he responded to our greeting saying, "Peace and all good… You're visiting at this hour?" We explained the reason for the delay and mentioned the difficulties the porter had created for us. Then, with a severe voice, he said, "Know that I still have my strength to go down and open the door for Mario and Adolfo." I was moved by this further expression of affection.

I approached him and introduced the man who asked for a blessing. Padre Pio gladly blessed him, adding, "And be a good Christian." Then as usual, not wanting to miss an opportunity, I asked, "Father, will

> "Father, will you promise me that you will bless everyone I present to you?" His response was firm, "Yes, now and when I'm gone."

you promise me that you will bless everyone I present to you?" His response was firm, "Yes, now and when I'm gone."

And this would be that cranky, rude monk with boorish manners as those who never even knew him sometimes described him? Instead, only someone who is deeply sensitive and profoundly spiritual could be so warm and accessible after an exhausting and tormenting day. Just consider for a moment how he walked on feet pierced by the wounds of the crucifixion all day long. Reason can go no further in trying to explain facts that must be accepted only by faith.

This is why our task is to open our hearts and accept that what Padre represented was God's gift to humanity as a mystery of the faith against ever-increasing atheism in the hearts of humanity. It is not up to us with our limitations, or through historical investigations that have little to do with holiness, to come up with a logical explanation of what happened through the person of Padre Pio.

Beginning on September 20, 1918, Padre was subject to numerous medical examinations. All confirmed the supernatural nature of his stigmata. For his beatification in 1999, the Church had to meticulously examine 104 volumes before issuing its pronouncement. Then there were many, many works [of miracles] desired by God through this beloved son of His.

It is not our task to explain why God impressed the seal of the crucifixion on this friar's body. We might say He did so to give us further confirmation of His presence among us. Or, perhaps He sought to tell us once again that He is the center of all of that exists -- not an unknowable God, but an assured presence through the figure of Christ who is none other than God Himself made man.

Those who do not accept this reality and do not recognize Padre Pio as a divine gift -- extended toward human suffering as a gift of himself -- are those who are often the first ones who desperately search for God, but are not able to open the door of their hardened hearts. "Behold I stand at the door and knock. If anyone hears my voice and opens there, I will come. I will dine with him and he with me" (Revelation 3:20).

How deaf and blind is humanity! People try to give an explanation of their existence and of all that is supernatural with the shortsightedness of reason, all the while ignoring the divine light that is already in their hearts. In the great game of life, "God is the One who seeks His creatures and at the same time is the One who allows Himself to be sought," as Cardinal Martini once said. Scripture says,

"You will seek me and find me. Because you seek me with all your heart, I will be found by you" (Jeremiah 29:13-14).

Do you, dear reader, recall what Padre Pio told me after Mass when I was staring at his stigmatized hands? "My son, these are things you cannot understand." Before that image of the living Christ there is only a response, "I believe." All we have to do is say, "I seek your face, O Lord." If we were to repeat these words often and with faith, so much more would be clearer, beginning with the mystery of the twentieth century: Padre Pio.

Andrea Bocelli, in concert at San Giovanni Rotondo for the first anniversary of the beatification of Padre Pio, gives homage to Padre Pio's remains.

FRANCA

I believe what follows is one of the last episodes [of intercession] that occurred after Padre's death. It was March, 2002 and Franca was having her usual checkup with her gynecologist in Rome, Dr. Liliana De Troia. Unbeknownst to us, that day was to be the beginning of a stormy period. Dr. De Troia ordered some tests as she sensed something was wrong. Indeed, the results of the tests revealed that Franca had ovarian cancer. You can imagine the despair we felt when we heard the bad news.

And so my wife underwent surgery on April 4, 2002 in the clinic of Santo Volto in Rome. We were assured that everything possible was being done to eliminate the possibility of metastases. Afterwards, she began a long and grueling recovery including chemotherapy.

Despite everything, however, I remained calm. I knew that Padre would make his presence felt, as he had promised. It was my task to be silent, to pray, and have a lot of faith. In fact, in my mind I could see the luminous figure of Padre supporting Franca during that terrible period. I could sense in the air that something strange was happening. And indeed it was.

Through the intercession of Padre Pio, the Omnipotence of God was fashioning the most peculiar of scenarios. On July 25, 2002, my sister, Lidia, was admitted to the hospital of the House for the Relief of Suffering in San Giovanni Rotondo for routine tests. Her roommate, Tina Ienco, was being treated for cancer.

One morning, Ms. Ienco woke up, looked at my sister, and said, "How strange. Last night I had a dream of Padre Pio. It was more than a dream; it seemed like a vision. He said to me, 'Tell my son, Adolfo, not to worry about his wife. In September, she'll be back home making homemade pasta.'"

113

My sister was shocked. She replied, "Adolfo is my brother. And his wife, in fact, just underwent an operation a few months ago." She called me right away and asked me to come to San Giovanni Rotondo. When I got there, she introduced me to Ms. Ienco whom I had never before met. She told me the same story and I choked up with natural emotion and gratitude for such special attention from Padre.

She then asked me to talk to her about my personal relationship with Padre Pio. As I was getting ready to leave, she said, "It's obvious that Padre Pio loves you very much." I nodded and returned home to Foggia. Before leaving, however, I embraced her in what was to be a final farewell. She died one year later after suffering terribly.

In November, 2003, Franca underwent another laparoscopy procedure in Monza [Northern Italy] performed by Dr. Mangioni, one of the best oncologist-gynecologists in Europe. At the end of the operation, lasting about four hours, the surgeon exited the operating room, approached me and said, "Mr. Affatato, everything is all right. I removed one last lump about 1 mm long. Do you know how I operated? With this image of Padre Pio in my gown pocket." He then pulled out a beautiful photograph of a smiling Padre Pio which instilled confidence. Yet another confirmation.

A few years later, on September 6, 2007, I took Franca to the doctor for her regularly scheduled check-up. This time, however, we were a little apprehensive as she was now in her fifth year of recovery. After a careful examination, Dr. Mangioni said, "Madam, you're doing great. Let's give thanks to God. Everything looks good and the worst is behind us. Of course, you should continue having periodic check-ups. By the way, did you know that I'll be coming down to San Giovanni Rotondo on September 26 to chair a meeting on oncology in Padre Pio's hospital?" By now, I had clearly discerned the presence of Padre. But the best was yet to come.

After leaving Dr. Mangioni's office, we walked to the train station. As usual, I prayed the Rosary to give thanks, which I always did during such times. But to my surprise I realized I did not have it with me. So once I was in the station, I went to a newsstand and asked if they had any rosary beads. Several bystanders looked at me somewhat strangely. (I wasn't surprised as people today have mostly lost a sense of the spiritual life and the need to pray.) Nonetheless, the woman on the other side of the counter said to me, "I don't believe I have any, but if you wait a minute, I'll see if I can find something in the drawer." She rummaged around and pulled out a little rosary with an image of Padre Pio. It was my sign. That afternoon, Padre Pio had not left us alone -- not even for a moment.

The words spoken to me so many years earlier resounded in all their relevance, "I will help you and I will assist you until the last moment of your life.

THE WAY OF LOVE

Padre Pio was an example of love and he gave of himself to all people with his entire heart. His whole life was an act of love toward God and others to the point that he said, "I will remain at the gates of heaven, until the last of my spiritual children enters." One example is that night when I told him at the end of my confession, "Father, I love you so much." Visibly moved, he said to me, "Obviously you do not know how much I love you."

In Galatians, St. Paul said, "As for me, may I never boast about anything except the cross of our Lord Jesus Christ, through which the world has been crucified to me, and I to the world... From now on, let no one cause me trouble, for I bear on my body the marks of Jesus" [Galatians 6:14,17]. It seems that the Apostle was describing what Padre Pio experienced many centuries earlier. However, unlike Paul in this Scripture, Padre Pio did not ask for people not to cause him trouble. Instead, Padre Pio gave himself to sinners and to all suffering souls in order to bring them close to the Heart of God.

People were created by an act of love of God. And God wants us to be witnesses to the love that is within us and to manifest it in every circumstance of our life. And this is the essence of life: we are life, we are light, we are love. Our life does not end with our earthly sojourn; instead, our soul is eternal and immortal.

Padre Pio loved the crucified Jesus so much that he asked for and received the marks of the crucifixion as a participant in the work of the redemption of mankind. I do not believe that anyone today can imagine the terrible and painful suffering which Padre endured in the name of the love he had for Christ -- that same love that led him to identification with God.

Certainly, from a perspective of logic, it is inconceivable that anyone would ask to suffer in the name of love to the point of being crucified. But I have already said that Padre Pio had little left of his humanity; instead, everything was divine. And we know that humanity, merely with the five senses, cannot explain what comes in the afterlife. There remains only the act of faith: believing. That's all.

But the sublimation of Padre Pio's love became truly heroic as his love extended to all suffering souls and sinful people who approached him. His saving intercession extended toward healing and redemption. Padre acted in this way only because his heart was full of love, which he poured out on all who came to him. He had the power to see beyond people's physical aspect: he looked into their souls, which were needy and hungry. They were eager to quench their thirst with his inexhaustible wellspring.

In Padre's every gesture, there was a need to serve God and neighbor, because he understood with his enlightened mind that the essence of life was in giving. Andrè Giole once wisely wrote in his diary, "Only when we are able to give do we truly possess. Everything we are not able to give possesses us."

This is why he was sometimes harsh toward those who offended the light of Christ within them through immorality or sacrilege. Yet, he offered himself as a victim even for those souls allowing God to fulfill everything else through His mercy. I heard him say countless times, "It will be done according to our faith; we will be judged based on love."

Here I would like to pause and focus on the concept of love in more general terms. When we return to the Father's House after our earthly journey, the only thing we will bring with us will be love. And the only thing people will leave on this earth is also love, inasmuch we have been able to love. And this is why love is the most beautiful gift of life; it gives meaning to it and makes it worth living.

We must first convince ourselves, however, that if we want to be loved, we ourselves must love. As did Padre Pio. He loved and did nothing else. Here I quote St. John once again, "I give you a commandment: love one another" [John 13:34]. Jesus invites us to love one another and He puts this teaching at the foundation of the spiritual life and as an explanation for how extraordinary things can happen to us in life. These sentiments are at the basis of the miracles of Padre Pio who was an endless source of love. Padre Pio prayed constantly, and he understood prayer as a continual giving of himself. Inasmuch as people are spiritual entities, people are the result of their acts of love. And this alone can change our destinies. The only true power in the world is the ability to love, because love makes the difference and can do all things.

When we say in the Our Father, "Thy Kingdom come," we are praying that the Kingdom of love be realized on earth. Here Jesus is referring to the true Kingdom of happiness in which all problems will be solved. In coming to earth, Jesus brought the law of love, which revolutionized the history of humanity.

An old adage says, "Love, and do what you wish" [St. Augustine]. And so it is that those who love have completely fulfilled the divine law. And those who truly love possess the other virtues necessary to love. Only by loving can we advance readily in spiritual progress, because love is expansion and in it we become spiritual forces at work.

Before us stands that spiritual giant, Padre Pio, who, by welcoming and loving all desperate creatures who turned to him, he enveloped them in that radiant divine light.

Therefore, we must free ourselves from this culture of egoism, because love -- the principle of life -- is the only way to salvation. When we are able to love even those who have offended us, we will have begun to implement that necessary change in our mentality and we will have passed from theory to practice. To truly love, we must have all the other virtues. For this, love is the highest summit of the spiritual life.

Love is an internal disposition of the mind and thought. It makes our hearts pulsate in union with God and with all creatures, because all things are in God and are a manifestation of Him. Love sees God easily in the most humble being and fulfills true brotherhood even there.

We must not fear that we will ever be given a burden beyond our strength.

We should fill our day with small acts of love: a smile, a word, a glance, a gesture, a handshake, a thought. Let these gestures be of comfort and help to those who need them. Let us enlighten our life and fill it with these little lights; otherwise, our lives will be filled with darkness.

When we do this, our lives will be transformed and we will bear light which will shine through our eyes and our words, but especially through the example of our lives. The light of God that is within us asks only to be unearthed from the accumulation of sins that have imprisoned it in order to be able to be filled with a new limitless joy.

We must become, in the words of St. Paul, a "temple of Christ living within us" [cf. 1 Cor 3:16]. We must be among those who are able to put in action, with love, the process of illumination of our own life. Then we will no longer need rules because we will have happily arrived at our destination. St. John of the Cross once said, "Here there is no more road, because for the just man there is no law. He is law unto himself," because when we reach that point, we will have identified with divinity, "The Father and I are one." The realization of the state of grace, which is reached by faith, love, and prayer will bring us to a conscious existence full of happiness.

I have dwelled at length on the concept of love here because Padre Pio's life was an act of total love toward God and toward others. Everything I have written in these pages is the fruit of my spiritual journey which began in 1953. And today my vision of life is exactly what you can read here in this little book. The sacrifice of Padre Pio must serve us as a guide if we wish to fulfill our true identities as children of God.

If we have not understood the law of love and have not applied it in our daily lives, we can never understand the true significance of the presence of Padre Pio among us. It is not enough to visit his tomb, or to go to Mass, or to pray if our minds have not been radically transformed. If this is all we do, it is only part of the duty of being a good Christian.

If we go home after our visit to San Giovanni Rotondo and close ourselves once again in selfishness and think only of cultivating our little garden, this is not enough. Instead, we must radically change the way we live. And this can be achieved only if we live a morally exemplary life on the spiritual path, and are led by the law of love that can do all things. Faith and love are the two essential elements that lead us directly to the Heart of God.

If our inner faith is not translated into daily practice, it will have been a waste of time. This is like fetching water from the fountain with a bucket with a hole in it; when we get home there will be no more water.

And so it is with the spiritual life. If we do not radically change course and if we return to our old ways, our journey toward our interior life will be very slow and fruits will be difficult. Once again, however, we find solace in faith.

Padre Pio is alive today -- he is in contact with our souls more than you can imagine.

Padre Pio is alive today -- just as yesterday. Of course we cannot see him physically, but I can guarantee you that today, as pure divine energy, he is in contact with our souls more than you can imagine.

He speaks to our hearts, because love is eternal and infinite.

All we have to do is descend into interior silence, pray, call upon him with faith, and then look with the eyes of the heart. Then we can rest assured that he will respond, especially when it comes to asking for help with the spiritual journey. Then we will see, as a miracle, the veils lifted up one by one presenting us with reality which we could not see previously. In the words of Alexis Carrel, "Prayer is the greatest strength in the world."

Everything I have written down here is the result of the maturation of my inner journey which began in 1953 under the direction of Padre Pio and continued after his ascension to heaven. Yet, even then I remained always under his protection which was even stronger than while he was alive on earth.

Over the course of my journey, I developed the following concepts and remain firmly convinced of them:

1) We must recognize the divine Presence within us as the only power that exists in the world;

2) We must honor and worthily represent this light within us.

We have the duty to be strict guardians of this divine heritage, as was Padre Pio, and we must constantly be vigilant so that the light never grows dim within us. We must do so in order to master and control the powerful world of emotions that surrounds us so that we remain firmly within God's grace. We must surrender control of our lives to divine love and ask for, yesterday as today, the intercession of our beloved Padre Pio. By mastering our little egos, we put into action the energy of the divine Presence. And then there is no obstacle that can stand in the way.

When we arise in the morning, we should invoke God to assist us throughout the day we are about to begin. We say, "May your light illuminate the way and may your love guide my steps." Then those you meet will then see someone who is serene and smiling, wise and loving, soft-spoken, gentle and sober. The divine light will emanate from within you.

The fifteen years I spent alongside Padre were the most beautiful in my life, and they bore much fruit. I say it again: even after his ascension to heaven, I have continued to enjoy and obtain guidance from Padre as I have experienced authentic and objective validations.

I would like to say a huge thank you to you, dear reader, for the gift of allowing me to write about Padre Pio who is not only mine, but is now also yours.

My hope is that my words, though scarce when confronted with the importance of this great saint, will penetrate the depths of your hearts. In the silence of your homes, in the recollection of your thoughts, in common purpose, I hope they will inspire you to arise and do most beautiful, noble and sublime things. And in your life journey I hope my words will be cause for you to lift your aspirations upwards, toward our Padre Pio, this sweet Padre Pio, who was crucified in his body while his face illuminated the arch of heaven.

This is the same Padre Pio who once said to me, but now says to you, "My children, I am close to you, closer than you can imagine. I am in contact with your mind and am directing your thoughts; I am close to your heart and am counting your heartbeats, so that with all in unison -- in perfect harmony of the universe -- they might lift up a hymn of glory to God the Father Almighty."

It is my wish now for all of you to cross beyond that door where there is so much serenity. There you will find the very meaning of life itself. When you have walked beyond that door, you will have found the way. Then all will seek you, because they will see in your eyes the way of ascent on high.

Love Padre Pio. He is the bridge between the finite and the infinite, between the human and the divine. He is light that shows the way all people can follow as long as their hearts are open.

Love him in the silence of your hearts. Love him in continuous and deep prayer. Love him by applying the law of love daily. But love him primarily by the witness of your life.

Now that I have told you my experiences as a spiritual son of Padre Pio, you can no longer say that you do not know of his divine essence and his heroic sacrifice for a suffering and sinful humanity. Now you know him as I do, and therefore you, too, have a duty, as I still do, to bear witness. When you have done this, he will take command of your life. Then your thoughts and feelings will be guided by the divine light and your life will look completely different. You will see what you did not see before; you will fulfill that which seemed impossible. Your hopes, your dreams, and your highest aspirations will be guided by his voice that speaks to your heart.

I leave you with the following thoughts which represent the summary of my inner journey under the direction of Padre Pio:

The mind is limited;
life is short.
Every good deed,
every smile,
every word of comfort,
which I wish
to give to you…
permit me to do so now.
Because life is an ascent
toward our true essence
as children of Divine Love
created to witness to this love.

Adolfo Affatato

Preface to the Second Edition

What follows is the Second Edition which was written after I [the author] exhausted all the copies from the first edition. [This new edition] was requested by many friends who read the first and it is made up of excerpts from various conferences I gave throughout Italy. The first section remains exactly as it was because it relates to my personal life with Padre Pio. In this new second section, there are reflections of those who saw, of those who heard.

Even so many years after I wrote what you are about to read, I felt pervaded by strong inner emotions, by feelings of love and gratitude to this great Saint, my spiritual father, the God-Man, who brought LIGHT and TRUTH into my life.

Even today, those who have had the occasion to listen to me, may notice that when I speak of some episodes about Padre which are still alive in my heart, I am deeply moved. During those times, I feel him pulsate within me; I feel every tear that bathes my face return to my heart and cause it to overflow of love. It is his love that caresses me. I hope this will happen to you and allow you to discover what you may have been looking for so long: the love of God.

Finally, I have copied some emails and testimonies below which I received. I hope that they may become food for meditation in that these people have rediscovered their faith through the Padre Pio they did not know and so many of them have [now] opened the door before which for some time Jesus, through Padre Pio, had been knocking in vain: The Door of Faith.

Most of all, I have been moved by the letter of a mother who lost her 18-year-old son and was in the throes of a suicidal depression. She said, "I found faith and the strength to go on." How strange the life of the spirit is sometimes! Through episodes that took place, described simply, Padre Pio touched the heart of this woman using an unlettered man such as myself.

Dear reader, if you are reading this book, there is a reason. Perhaps there is a message in it that Padre Pio wishes to say directly to you. If, however, [this book] shall be destined to accumulate dust on a shelf somewhere, then give it to someone else, for it could be a great gift for that person. It may be that Padre Pio wishes to talk to them to open the doors of their heart.

For everyone, I wish for serenity of mind, love and charity of heart, and health of body so that all may witness with our lives the presence of God in us that is the theme of this book.

Adolfo Affatato

As a coral draws lifeblood from the sea,
so I drew from Padre Pio every word and
every thought that could enrich me evermore.

In the end, my "Our Father" emerged
with commentary which I recite daily,
slowly, and in deep meditation.

It allows me to feel more secure and confident
in dealing with the day.
I hope the same for you.

OUR FATHER

Our Father who art in heaven
(On earth, in every place, because there where life where -- there You are...
with Your omnipresence, omnipotence, omniscience)

Hallowed be thy name.
(Yes Father, by invoking Your Holy Name in the silence of my soul, make me
be fulfilled in You. And You, good Father, can take possession of my body and
my soul so that I will represent You worthily in this earthly sojourn)

Thy kingdom come
(May Your Kingdom, O Father, comprised of peace, love, harmony)

Thy will be done on earth as it is in heaven.
(O Father, may Thy will be done, not mine because You alone know what I
do not know, You alone see what I do not see, You alone know if what I desire
is good and right for me. So, Father, may Thy will be done, the only one that
can give me peace and serenity)

Give us this day our daily bread.
(Give me, Father, serenity for my mind, love and charity for my heart, and
health for my body. Help my soul to understand what I need for a balanced
and serene life)

And forgive us our trespasses as we forgive those who trespass against us.
(Father, forgive the sins my human frailty makes me commit, just as I have

the duty to forgive those who offend me. Forgive me, Father, for my lack of self-esteem, forgetting your presence within me)

And lead us not into temptation.
(Father, cloak me in your paternal love protecting me in moments of weakness so that I do not fall into sin; illuminate, Father, my earthly journey with Your Divine Light)

But deliver us from evil. Amen.
(Father, the greatest evil I could commit would be to forget you even for one moment during the day. Cast away from me feelings of anger, resentment, and hatred. Have me replace these with love and forgiveness. Have me, Father, say in every moment, "I live, I move, I exist in God who manifests Himself within me at all times.")

Thus I hope. Thus may be it be.

Adolfo Affatato

I STAND AT THE DOOR

On the occasion of this second edition of my book, it is my desire to share all the practical and concrete lessons I have learned from the teachings of Padre Pio in my daily life with all my many friends who read the first edition. And here, at the outset, I would like to state that I, the writer, am a layperson, and, moreover, very pragmatic. All the same, I had the fortune of perhaps seeing farther than others because I stood on the shoulders of a giant of the Church: a humble friar who rests today in the Heart of Almighty God. For this reason, my writings are often inclined toward the undertakings of daily life.

As a result of my journey, I have become a positive person. I am aware that I am not alone, but am intimately connected to the divine light within me. And this is due solely to Padre Pio. From the first moment when I encountered him and he told me, "I have been waiting for you for a long time," he formed me based on the ways of God the Father. In his goodness, perhaps he saw something good in me.

Perhaps you have seen a certain painting by Caravaggio in the church of St. Louis of France in Rome. Known as, "The Calling of St. Matthew," it takes place in an eating establishment in which Matthew is intent on playing dice with some friends. In the throes of the game, Matthew's right hand clearly resting on some coins, Jesus enters. He is accompanied by St. Peter who stands leaning on a walking stick, representative of the itinerant Church.

Jesus extends his index finger toward Matthew in an act of calling him. At that moment, Matthew is illuminated by the divine light of conversion, while the others remain still in the shadows. Two players, in fact, even continue to count their money all the while ignoring the presence of Jesus; they symbolize attachment to worldly things, blindness to the spiritual life, and blocked contact with God.

Matthew's reaction is touching: he points to himself seemingly expressing his incredulity at being chosen personally by the Lord. Yet, Jesus again confirms that it is He who calls, as St. John says, "You have not chosen me, but I have called you" [John 15:16]. We have only one duty: to be fertile ground when the grain falls in order to bear fruit and bear it abundantly. If you have never seen "The Calling of St. Matthew, it's worth doing so, you'll love it!

This painting reminds me of my own calling when Padre Pio called me by name from among a crowd of people. I, too, asked in disbelief, "But Father, do you mean me?" And without ever having met me before, as if the most natural thing in the world, he quipped, "Is my name, by chance, Adolfo?"

"The Calling of St. Matthew" -- Caravaggio

The law of the spirit has remained unchanged over time, even after many centuries. It is we who are so often arid of heart. And after my "solemn investiture," I pledged to continuously try to be a worthy spiritual son of Padre Pio. And I have strived -- and still strive -- to bring Padre's true image whenever I am called to speak about him.

I am reminded of the miracle St. Peter worked for the paralytic man before the Temple. Scandalized by what happened, the high priests summoned St. Peter and asked for an explanation [cf. Acts: 3-4]. They requested that he no longer speak of Jesus as the Messiah, the longed-for Son of God. But Peter's answer was simple, "We have been guided by the Spirit of Christ who has worked in us… It is impossible for us not to speak about what we have seen and heard" [cf. Acts 4:19-20].

And today, his spiritual children and those who were witnesses to him have an obligation to speak to posterity about what happened. Therefore, what follows are reflections that have come spontaneously to my mind about this great saint who still calls over five million pilgrims each year to San Giovanni Rotondo.

Those who come are hungry for faith and thirsty for light. They are often lost and afraid in this society which has seen a plunge in moral values. They seek peace and an inner serenity which the world has denied them -- this same world that worships technology on its altar, all the while forgetting that humanity has a spirit as well as a human body that must be fed.

When I speak to groups, I like to give the following example. I say, "We are all *cappuccini* [i.e. Capuchin friars]." I then explain that when we go to the coffee bar and order a cappuccino, we can no longer distinguish the milk from the coffee; we drink one cappuccino. Similarly, the nature of man is made up of both a human and a spiritual component. However, we often forget about the spiritual side and look after only the human part.

Padre Pio did not do this. In him, there was practically nothing left of his humanity because he was so completely spiritual and illuminated. He was a spiritual being having a human experience. I have no other way to explain how he lived for fifty years as a crucified man and walked on feet pierced as with nails. He was like Saint Paul in his Letter to the Galatians, "I have been crucified in Christ, and is no longer I who live, but Christ lives in me" [cf. 2:20].

At the end I have copied some emails I received after a brief appearance on *Porta a Porta*. [Tr.: Porta a Porta {"Door to Door"} is a well-known and reputable nightly Italian talk show hosted by Bruno Vespa on prime-time television.] They were sent to me by people who read the stories about my life, written in a simple but touching manner. Through the intercession of Padre Pio, the stories brought many people to the Heart of God. I must say how unworthy I feel in all this. Yet, I thank the Almighty for all the mercy he had for me, the miserable earthly creature that I am.

My experiences with Padre Pio have allowed me to show you the friar in his everyday humanity, completely permeated with divinity. My stories will invite you to meditate deeply on the great mystery of faith, a gift of God, which He, in His great goodness, never denies anyone who seeks it with all their will: "Behold! I stand at the door and knock. If anyone hears my voice and opens the door, I will come in and dine with him and he with me" [Revelation 3:20].

If I had to describe Padre Pio today based on my experiences with him, I would say he was, "A crucified man who lived on Earth for the redemption of sinners and for the relief of suffering humanity."

His life mission was the confessional: through this daily ministry, he attracted souls to himself, emptied them of all sin, shaped them according to the will of God and made them authentic witnesses of the gospel. All those who placed themselves under his illuminated direction received assistance -- tangible and practical even in the events of daily life, as happened to me.

Due to his teachings, the word "fear" is no longer a part of my vocabulary and I never feel alone. Even today, as an invisible, but genuine, guide, he shows me the right way and leads me in the best direction. As I have already said, I have become a positive person who always sees the glass half full and never half empty. I know that the sun is always there shining behind every cloud. Behind every problem, there is a solution that must be sought and discovered within. Behind every obstacle we may encounter there is always a source of growth.

From Padre Pio I learned the following:

- *To look at the bright side of everything*
- *To wish happiness to everyone I meet*
- *To never hold a grudge against anyone and to forgive always*
- *To always be serene and to offer a smile to those who do not know how to smile*
- *More than anything else, I learned that saying the magic word "Love" leads directly to the Heart of God.*

Therefore, let us offer love first of all to God for what He gives us, and let us gratefully acknowledge all we have received. Then let us say it to our friends, relatives, children and to everyone we meet.

People desire love out of existential necessity. We all want love, and when we say, "I love you" to someone, a certain energy emerges from us which others perceive immediately. And it was that energy and happiness that emanated from Padre Pio who continuously said, "My God, I love you." His love was immeasurable beyond the confines of human logic.

Darkness is the absence of light, it is obvious that we turn our backs to the light. Instead, if we enter a room and turn on the light switch, the room lights up. And so it is within our soul: if we turn on the switch of faith, the light goes on inside us. It illuminates our heart, our mind, and our entire being; it spreads everywhere we go and is transmitted to all those we encounter. This was the divine essence of Padre Pio who worked for the good of humanity each day.

Next, there is the second part of my description of Padre Pio: "Relief of suffering humanity." When the Hospital of the House of the Relief of Suffering was almost complete, it was noted that it was probably too luxurious what with all the marble. However, Padre Pio quickly and shrewdly replied, "If I had it my way, I would have made even the beds out of gold, because where the patient is, the living Christ is." The House of Relief was unquestionably his beloved creation. It was a place where people suffering in body and soul could look to him with a glimmer of hope.

Yet, the Most High did not always grant miracles -- not even to Padre Pio who was so beloved to the Heart of God. No one knows why as such things are a mystery beyond the human mind which cannot understand the divine plan.

Here I am reminded of what took place during the month of August, 1962. My father fell ill and was diagnosed with stomach cancer within a few days. Naturally, I immediately went to Padre Pio and asked him to intercede. I shall never forget his response, "My son, leave him be where he is. Life is good and is not ours. We are born naked and we die more naked still. If I could have, I would have saved my own mother from her death. We must lower ourselves to the will of God. But I promise you that when he goes to Heaven, I will be close to him. And this will take place in one day that is dear to me."

After I returned to Foggia, despite what Padre had told me, my siblings decided to take our father to a hospital in Rome by ambulance so as to have exhausted every possibility. So late at night on August 9, I left with my father accompanied by my sister-in-law, Rina Costantini, who was a nurse, and a physician, Dr. Parente.

When we were in Formia [Tr.: halfway between Rome and Naples] at 5:00 am on August 10 -- a date most dear to Padre Pio (as it was the day of his priestly investiture) -- my sister-in-law, who was seated next to my father and the doctor in the back seat, called out to me saying, "Adolfo have the driver stop the ambulance; your father is not doing well." I was seated in the front beside the driver who promptly stopped the car. I immediately got out and climbed into the back. At that moment, we all smelled the fragrance of roses strongly. At that very moment, Padre Pio was celebrating Mass in San Giovanni Rotondo. I had just enough time to embrace my father who then died in my arms.

When I returned to San Giovanni Rotondo I went to Padre Pio who said to me, "My son, I could not do any more than that. I accompanied his soul to Heaven." On hearing these words, though I was feeling tremendous pain and suffering because, among other things, we were ten children who were now without a father, I was nonetheless filled with a sense of peace, serenity and confidence in the future.

From that moment onward, Padre Pio took me even more under his guidance and protection in a beautiful way extending to me his closeness even during the most human of life events.

That experience left its mark on me. From it, I realized that there are moments in this life when we feel a particular affinity with the sacred -- with that divine spark within us. These are times when the heavens seem to stoop down toward our fleshly bodies with the angels who come to assist us. They are times of great difficulty when we face the major battles of life -- when it seems as if we are alone and helpless in the wake of the trials we must face. These are the times when Padre Pio places his crucified hands on our heads and tells us, "My son, have faith; I am at your side."

I know that Padre Pio always generously reciprocates his affection a hundred-fold, because his is a divine love -- a universal love that is boundless and limitless, and it sustains the entire universe. It comes from a great God who listens and loves everyone.

Presenting the book in Putignano (Bari) with Pinuccio Vinella (on the left).

134

THE POWER OF INNER CALM

When in the presence of Padre, it was natural to lower your voice. Not out of fear, but because when you were near him, his silence was more deafening than thunder. A power emerged from his heart and eyes... a divine presence that took in everything. It was inexplicable. You felt suffused with a sense of inner peace and joy such that at a certain point it seemed like your heart would explode with happiness. "Around him everything was light, everything was love, everything was indescribable inner peace." As time went by, that prayerful whispering at my soul and the light within me began to take shape under his wise and enlightened direction. I became more and more aware of the unfolding of the divinity within.

Though I have already written a chapter dedicated to his long silences, I would like to use this occasion to focus more on this aspect of Padre. Some silences are powerful in their inner stillness -- like those apparent long silences of his in which he prayed one rosary after the other in constant communication with God. He was like St. Paul who wrote to the Corinthians, "I, for my part, although absent in body but present in spirit" [1 Cor 5:3]. It was natural to dream endlessly during those long silences that completely enveloped me. It felt like a miracle: the mind and body were cloaked in a sense of peace, and frustrations and daily worries vanished.

In our present age, everything is so fast-paced that no one has time anymore. There is no time to smile; to offer others a smile; to show people we encounter that there is something in them that pulsates; to wish for everyone to have serenity and happiness; to remember that we are a temple of that divine spark that does not allow us to get carried away by anger; to be too happy to create problems. Above all, we do not have time to: "Meditate, Pray, and Love."

Instead, we must spiritualize our bodies and convince ourselves that we are channels blessed by God and created to serve our neighbor. We must, in essence, become bridges between humanity and God. Then, we will have realized the true meaning of our earthly existence.

Chilo, one of the seven sages of ancient Greece, was once asked what the hardest thing in life was. He replied simply: SILENCE.

In fact, the forces of humanity tend toward agitation, toward a disordered and selfish expression in the exterior world. Silence, on the other hand, is part of self-mastery over these forces in superior equilibrium. Yet, those who are still disturbed by strong emotions have difficulty achieving it. This is why silence is so often difficult.

Here, the Gospel of Matthew is applicable, "Let your 'Yes' mean 'Yes,' and your 'No' mean 'No.' Anything more is from the evil one" [5:37]. It follows that the only alternative to silence is the word which alone can bring comfort or do good. And herein is the wonderful result: there is no loss of energy but rather a continuous reciprocation; in fact, the more one gives, the more one receives. As Pascal says, "He is worth nothing who benefits no one."

And this is precisely what happened to Padre Pio. He did not preach sermons; he spoke with his crucified body. His every word pulsated from one soul to the next. His speech penetrated deep into the hearts of those who approached him and then rose up in the immensity of the infinite heavens to bring comfort to all those who were desperate and were looking for a safe haven, an inner peace lost.

Vico of Varo once said, "Speak with your actions; work without saying anything; act without opening your mouth. Say with facts what others say with their tongues. This alone has value."

Padre Pio translated his words into action daily. One might say, as those who knew him like I did, that everything in him was love, everything was divinity at the service of others.

Each day, so many of us ask ourselves what life can offer us in order for us to be happier and what we can do to avoid life's difficulties. Yet, practically no one asks what they could do to improve society.

We don't have to do monumental things; we just have to include noble causes in our way of life and in the goals that we pursue. We are not asked to be exceptional like Padre Pio with his suffering or like Mother Teresa of Calcutta who embraced lepers in the name of Christ. Rather, we are simply to be like a silent angel who does good in the world or someone who is fully aware of the divine love within that he proclaims to the society where he lives -- not with great words, but with great actions that leave footprints which time cannot erase.

Here I would like tell you a story that happened recently. After my appearance on the talk-show, *Porta a Porta*, a woman from Ostia [Tr.: a city on the Tyrrhenian Sea near Rome] named Leila, got a hold of my book through my sister, Teresa. She said that her 10-year-old son, Gabriel, was sick with leukemia.

After a few months she called me and said, "Sir, thank you for the book you sent me. I read it all in one sitting. Actually, I devoured it. If you only knew how much serenity you have given me. Gabriel asks me to re-read it to him continuously. He says that every time he hears it, he feels Padre Pio close to him. If you only knew how much happiness all this gives me. I do not know if my child will live or die, but today I am thankful to Padre Pio and to you, because with your simple language you have touched the heart of my son and you gave him so much serenity and hope." At that moment I felt unworthy. If she had been standing in front of me I would have kissed her feet.

Anna Galli, the leader of a Padre Pio prayer group, during the presentation of my book in Corinaldo (Ancona).

At a later time, I went to Ostia to hold a conference hosted by a Padre Pio Prayer Group. At the end of my talk, Gabriel appeared in the back of the church with his mother who had gone to the hospital to get him so I could meet him. You can imagine what I felt in that encounter. I held him tightly to my chest and told him not to worry saying, "Padre Pio loves you and is always close to you."

He stared at me with two big eyes -- marked by illness, yet full of life -- and said, "Adolfo, can I ask you for a favor? Please tell Padre Pio to look after my hospital roommate and friend, Francesco, who is ill." I assured him I would definitely do so. I embraced him once again and we said goodbye.

You gave me such a lesson in life, Gabriel. Thank you.

I hope, dear reader, that you will always remember Gabriel's story. And when it seems as if everything is going wrong in your life, ask if you have the right to complain. Ask if you should always think about what you want instead of giving thanks to God for what you have.

Smile and be grateful always. You have many reasons to be thankful. Smile more. God loves those who give of themselves with a smile. Smile always. Smile at everyone. Smile at everything. In the smile, more than one would believe, the expressive grace of true Love is present which is the gift of Himself. And the more you give it, the more God will manifest Himself within you. Then the miracle will take place: everyone you meet will see the light of the divine presence shining in your eyes.

Inauguration of the chapel of Padre Pio in Santa Anna
with funds received from the first edition.

DARE SOMETHING WORTHY

Aude aliqvid dignum. This Latin expression meaning, "Dare something worthy," is special to me, also for the fact that Padre Pio modelled his own life after it from his childhood onward. In fact, he set out to place himself in harmony with the mind of God.

What does it mean to think with the mind of God? Being filled with the Holy Spirit, living in full awareness of the presence of God in oneself -- that same God who had taken possession of the body of Padre Pio to the point of accomplishing so many things that were illogical and supernatural: healing the sick, enlightening people's minds so they could see with the eyes of God that which was not possible to human eyes, or perform an act or utter a word that could not be explained with human logic. God has no limits.

Imagine for a moment what your life would be like if you thought like God and if you were in harmony with His universal mind. What would you worry about? *Absolutely nothing.*

All we have to do is allow deep faith to take root in us. This will lead us to achieve all we desire ("If you have faith as a mustard seed, nothing is impossible" [cf. Matthew 17:20; Luke 17:6]). This must become the first and true meaning of our lives: the commencement of a new spiritual life, the beginning of a new journey which has the Heart of God as its goal.

Let us never forget to express our gratitude for all life has given us. We recall Socrates who once said, "He who is not content with what he has, will not be content with what he shall have."

Padre Pio demonstrated that how all things helped create the interior silence that brought him the peace that only God the Father could have given him: prayer; the conversion of souls; the acceptance of suffering in the name of Christ who came to Earth to save mankind; and the strength to endure humiliations (the most serious of which was his prohibition to celebrate Mass in public and the consequent ban on having contact with his spiritual children).

Modern man, on the other hand, does not have peace within. People today are all too often distracted by the daily demands of life and are confused by their mental thoughts which are so often in turmoil. Further, their hearts are emptied and so many are lost in the midst of the desert of loneliness. How can they ever find God?

Padre Pio was at one with himself spiritually in the solitude of his cell. There was only peace and quiet there. There was his great secret, "The presence of God." His heavy step, the continuous prayers he whispered that penetrated the Heart of God -- these were the poignant secrets of a man in continuous ecstasy that had taken full possession of his body pierced by the Blood of Christ.

Those, like me, who were nourished by his love that reflected the infinite love of God were fortunate to be able to transform their lives. And the greatest act of love of Padre Pio was in becoming a living crucified man for the redemption of sinners and the relief of suffering humanity.

When we live in love, we enter within the true meaning of life; we enter in the dimension of light. Then every gesture and every word are illuminated to the point of penetrating the profundity of the heart from which there is no return. St. Paul wrote to the Ephesians, "For everything exposed by the light becomes visible, as everything that becomes visible is light" [5:13-14].

But is there proof of knowing when this light takes hold of our hearts? Of course there is! When there is peace in our hearts, happiness, and joy of living; when we know how to offer a smile to all we meet; when we know how to truly love everyone; when we abandon every sense of anger, bitterness and resentment. Then we will have the proof that God lives in us. "I will be with you until the end of time" [Matthew 28:20].

Let us call God by name. And His name is: LOVE. Let us say to Him with all our strength, "Lord, I love you." This is our first duty, as Padre Pio once wrote to Father Benedetto saying that his heart had become a volcano of love.

As I already mentioned in another part of the book, we [spiritual sons] often used to pass time in the sitting room adjacent to Padre's cell after evening prayer services. There he would relax, and from time to time he would even tell jokes. Yet, he never put down his rosary which was his direct line to his "Heavenly Momma," who was, in his own words, the real author of the miracles attributed to him.

Presentation in Francavilla a Mare.
Dr. Baldassarre Saverio, Franca (the author's wife), and Father Guglielmo Alimonti.

One evening, his voice breaking with emotion, he said that there were no words to describe the beauty of the Virgin, "Every time I see her, I remain in ecstasy." Similarly, St. Augustine once said, "Every miracle that God grants passes through the Blessed Virgin."

At the end of our meeting when I approached him to tell him good night, I noticed he was particularly emotional. He said to me, "My son, give the love that I have put in your heart to all those to whom you draw near. Because in this is the meaning of life."

How profound were those words! They encapsulated the meaning of our life for all people. There is no love more sacred than that which a father has for a son. In that moment, I felt that Padre Pio was no longer my spiritual father, but rather the true Father who was conveying to me such a strong emotion directly from Heaven. It is in love and gratitude that the doors of faith are opened. It is faith that brings us directly into the Heart of God, the merciful and attentive Father who is always attentive to our needs.

Unfortunately for us, however, it is often difficult to talk to God. Often, the plant of love that bears fruit and fruit in abundance is lacking, among other things. It is that same love which Padre Pio placed in my heart that night to give to all of you.

Among the many emails I received (some of which are published at the end of this book) is one sent by Prof. Nazareno Gabrielli. He is an expert in the Diocesan Tribunal for the Cause of Saints, and he led the exhumation of the remains of Padre Pio in 2008. Among other things, he asked me, "But why would Padre Pio choose you among so many other equally deserving people?"

Some answers are given directly in Scripture, "Jesus went up on a mountainside and called to him those he wanted, and they came to him. He appointed twelve …" (Mark 3:13-14). St. John said, "You did not choose me, but I chose you and appointed you so that you might go and bear fruit--fruit that will last" (15:16). St. Ambrose once said, "It is not man who finds the truth; rather, he must let the truth find him." All this means that Jesus calls those He wants not in accordance with human logic, but according to the context of a spiritual plan.

Thus, for us mere mortals it is difficult to understand the measure underlying such choices. Nonetheless, we have only one duty: to answer the call. Then we will become a wonderful expression of a life without end. For we do not seek God with the eyes of flesh, but with humility and purity of heart.

For once, let us put words aside and speak with our hearts. It is there where one finds the truth of all things; there is the energy that shows us the way forward. For the light of God shines within the heart that is serene and sincere. His voice becomes clearer and more audible when we gather in silence without uttering a word and instead think about the greatness and goodness of a loving and merciful God.

Talk to Padre Pio who is inside you. Because now he is light and love. He is divine love that is eternal and infinite. There is a part of us that is without time and there is a part of us that is without limits.

When we descend within ourselves in profound meditation with our minds turned to the Most High, there are no longer limits on our actions, nor time that can affect our plans. "For a thousand years in your eyes are like yesterday gone by, as a watch that passes in the night" (Psalm 90:4). In that moment, all becomes nothing and darkness becomes light. Then all problems have their solution within, not outside of us. This is another important aspect of the life of Padre Pio.

St. Luke once said, "Can the blind lead the blind? Will not both fall into a pit? No disciple is greater than his teacher; but when fully trained, every disciple will be like his teacher" [6:40]. Padre Pio was well prepared in the school of his Teacher, Jesus. Through his crucifixion, he had become like the Teacher, the true light bringing souls into the Heart of God.

A conference with the Rotary Club in Foggia with
Father Gerardo Saldutto and the president, Dr. Paolo Di Carlo.

143

Padre Pio and I

BELIEVING IS SEEING

People have been educated and raised with the rigid laws of logic and rationality including the principle, "Seeing is believing." In short, according to this principle, we believe only in what we can understand and verify. However, the many miracles and so many [supernatural] things that surrounded Padre Pio go beyond our limited human minds defying all logic and rationality. In the simplicity of daily life filled with much prayer and love for a suffering and sinful humanity, extraordinary events took place.

In order to enter the [spiritual] realm where all things are possible, we must learn to go beyond our rational mind and enter the dimension of spirituality. Through this [dimension], we become aware of our spiritual nature; that is, our soul that is part of our body. We must, in other words, understand that we are first and foremost spiritual beings and that life is a continuous interplay between the visible and invisible. We need to get in touch with our interior world, which is comprised of thought, feeling, imagination and intuition.

Being spiritual is to reduce our reliance on the five senses and develop a deep faith in something that is within us but which we will never experience with logic alone. In the Letter to the Hebrews, St. Paul wrote, "Faith is confidence in what we hope for and assurance in what we do not see" (11:1). When we have made contact with the divine presence that is within us, then we will have made the transition from physical beings having a spiritual experience to spiritual beings having a human experience.

Padre was a mediator, a channel, and a bridge between Heaven and Earth. Through him, the earthly life was transcended in the hereafter. By emptying himself of his human nature, he had full knowledge that the grace and the omnipotence of God was acting through him.

145

He was a kind of prelude -- a sort of preface -- to the true life guided by the Holy Spirit omniscient of God, enlightened by divine light. He was full of light. His every gesture and his every word were composed by the divine self which had taken possession of his body. The infinite love of God had completely enveloped the earthly life of Padre Pio. The divine and omniscient spirit was in him, and he was in the spirit.

From the moment I met him, the truest and greatest miracle was in my awareness of the unfolding of the divinity within me. We cannot give away what we do not have. If we allow the light of God's love to enter within our hearts, then we can liberate within others all the splendor of divine grace that is within them. Then our souls will be filled with the love of God and our eyes will shine with the light which will attract all those who come to us.

When the love and harmony of God determine our life, all our grudges and inner negativity will disappear as if a miracle. If love and inner peace guide our daily lives, then all our ways will become ways of joy and happiness. This will lead to a sense of complete satisfaction such as to make us say, "I live, speak and act in God who manifests himself within me at all times."

Padre Pio was sweetness and divine grace at the same time; he was a father and a brother; he was kind and good, but also strict when necessary. Seated in silence, he radiated love. And in this silence our conversations took place from heart to heart.

Padre taught me that God not only hears our prayers, but He knows our needs even before we begin to formulate them. And He is always ready to answer them. But in His omniscience, God sees the past, present and future. Therefore, He knows our eternal needs and He always answers our prayers in His immeasurable love according to our needs in terms of eternity. We need only have faith and patience, abandoning ourselves to His will.

The ingratitude of man from birth to death causes God to suffer very much. Through Padre's teachings, I understood that gratitude is an eternal virtue. The more we thank God for what happens to us, the more we create the conditions for further blessings. God desires nothing more, and in our turn, we will become like angels ready to help those in need. The fuel that feeds the divine light that shines within us is love, prayer and faith with the conviction that "God dwells within," as St. Paul says [cf. Romans 8:11].

While I was with Padre, I felt enveloped by an intense serenity. I felt so much love radiating from his figure and at the same time I felt so much joy in being close to him from whom I absorbed peace and happiness. And the knowledge that he, Padre, loved me so much filled me with such joy that I felt happily excited. Through Padre Pio, I felt the unconditional love of God. It was an infinite love that went beyond the earthly; it was a love he radiated to all his children.

Today, I realize just how much I was nourished by Padre's love by being close to him. His love was infinite, and I was literally immersed within it. And this is our true essence. Therefore, our first duty is to be witnesses of this love, opening ourselves in a flash of love toward everyone and everything. And, believe me, I was an eye witness, reaping the abundant fruit of the love of God which He poured out on me through Padre Pio.

My experience [with Padre Pio] is important only to the extent that it can open your hearts to love. Everything else is like a side dish. My mission is to apply Jesus' message, "Love one another as I have loved you" [John 15:12]. Try it, it doesn't cost anything.

God expresses Himself through His creation: creation and God are one. And Padre Pio was a masterpiece of the divine creation, a true work of art, which in this case assumes the name of holiness.

To find God means to journey within the self, as Padre Pio did, with a life in perfect harmony with the perfection that is already in our true essence as children of God through a continuous witness of the One who lives within us. To find God means to encounter peace and bliss, which lead as the final result to a life full of harmony, with a perfect balance between outward expression and inner peace.

When we embark on the most wonderful journey one can take -- that is toward God -- we will end up discovering a surprising result: ourselves. We ourselves are the beginning and end of our search: the alpha and the omega, the cause and effect of everything that happens to us.

That which we desire to achieve is already within us, because God who is omnipresent, omnipotent and omniscient is already present within us to the extent which we become aware of this reality. The principle of evolution and creativity that is within humanity is a spiritual principle.

When Jesus said, "The Father and I are one," [John 10:30] it means that the Spirit of God that was in Him is the same that is in all people. Padre Pio was aware of this spiritual energy that went beyond all possible imagination; it was also in him. Then, through a life of prayer and continual meditation, living life crucified, he made the divine gifts he received available to humanity. He was a bridge between people and God. At the same time, he was protagonist, actor and spectator of all the miracles the Most High worked through him.

People are essentially spiritual beings, and their relationship with God is similar to that of sunlight and the sun. The great power that each person possesses is in realizing that they are a temple of the spirit of God within them.

Padre's serenity completely enveloped me, and he gave me so much happiness that my heart was always full of joy. And his greatest joy was in giving all people the hope of experiencing God.

Through our free will, we create our own destiny. Life creates events which follow our thoughts and sentiments. Feelings of peace, love, harmony and joy follow positive thoughts, and positive events follow these; on the other hand, feelings of fear, depression, envy, resentment, and hatred follow negative thoughts, and these produce negative events.

DESIRE FOR GOD

We are all, more or less, aware of the need to get closer to God within ourselves; that is, to give a spiritual dimension to the body and, as a result, to channel the spirit. However, there is an obstacle we must overcome in this journey: the "ego," which is selfishness and rationality. We are selfish because we are ignorant, and we are often more dazzled by appearances than being. And all the while, we forget that God expresses Himself through His creation. And what creation is more noble and sublime than Padre Pio -- that worthy representative of all divine values that are in all men even if developing?

This was the last wedding celebrated by Padre Pio.
Printed with approval of the Archives of the Capuchin Fathers.

If people were aware of the incredible potential they have within themselves which if they could just bring to light, they would be astounded. St. Catherine of Siena once said, "If you become what you should be, you would set Italy ablaze." To this I would add, "You would set the world ablaze," as did Padre Pio.

When Jesus said, "The Father and I are one," it also applies to us in that we human beings, inasmuch as we are children of God, are made in His image. Yet, often we do not have the faintest idea of the potential that lies within us. It is well known that we utilize only ten percent of our capacity. "Whoever believes in me will do the works that I do, and will do greater ones than these" [John 14:12].

In light of these reflections, allow me to share the thoughts of Padre Pio who said that he himself marveled at being considered the worker of miracles. "What do you want from me? I'm just a friar who prays," was the phrase he used to say hiding behind an innocent smile.

Padre Pio knew that by emptying himself of his human nature, his sanctified body had become a source of love and of divine omnipotence. In fact, he once said to his confessor -- when asked for an explanation of what was said during colloquies with the Virgin Mary, "And you don't speak with Our Lady?" How pure and innocent were his words.

This was the last wedding celebrated by Padre Pio.
Printed with approval of the Archives of the Capuchin Fathers.

For Padre Pio, such supernatural experiences were the most normal thing in the world, just like my first encounter with him. The first time he called me, without me ever having seen him before, I asked incredulously, "Father, are you calling me?" And he naturally responded, "Is my name, by chance, Adolfo?" By then his body, which was filled with the light of the Holy Spirit, had become a safe haven for the suffering, for sinners seeking redemption, and for all who desired the serenity denied them by our fast-paced technology-driven society.

> Without me ever having seen him before, I asked incredulously, "Father, are you calling me?" And he naturally responded, "Is my name, by chance, Adolfo?"

This is such an important element which I must clarify to put everything in perspective: first and foremost Padre Pio took everything to God who was the sole author of everything that happened through him. He considered himself merely a mediator to the Merciful Heart of the Most High, the Creator of all that is. I shall never tire of saying this, as his unworthy spiritual son, so that you can have an understanding of who Padre Pio really was: a powerful intercessor to the Heart of God for our every need. This is what I feel I must tell you.

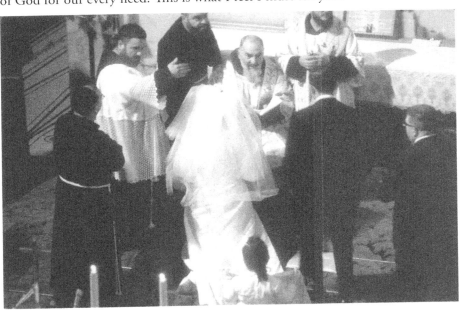

This was the last wedding celebrated by Padre Pio.
Printed with approval of the Archives of the Capuchin Fathers.

He resolutely would not allow anyone to consider him to be the worker of miracles. For this reason, he refused all forms of fanaticism and idolatry. This is why he was often very harsh especially toward those who tried to cut off a piece of his cord or tunic to take away as a relic. In this, he was like Jesus, "Jesus withdrew with his disciples to the lake, and a large crowd from Galilee followed. Because of the crowd he told his disciples to have a small boat ready for him, to keep the people from crowding him. For he had healed many, so that those with diseases were pushing forward to touch him" (Mark 3:7; 9-10).

And he was equally stern with unrepentant sinners who did not understand the opportunity God was offering them. For these reasons, those who said Padre Pio was too severe have not understood anything; or, they too have something within that needs to be forgiven.

But when confronted with humanity's ingratitude -- from birth to death -- God knows how to wait (as Padre Pio told me one day) until people discover their true nature as a creature made in God's image and likeness. Then comes the recognition of the inner light that has the power to change lives. Then we become aware, under the enlightened guidance of Padre, that God, the Creator of our

This was the last wedding celebrated by Padre Pio.
Printed with approval of the Archives of the Capuchin Fathers.

lives, has sought us since birth, but never found us at home. Instead, we were too far from the innermost part of our hearts; we were running around overwhelmed by the rhythm of life, forgetting that He was knocking at the door. Yet, we did not open for Him; we never devoted a small part of our day to Him.

Dear friends who are reading my book, with my heart wide open, based on the teachings I received from Padre Pio, I plead for you to, "Stop, be quiet, think, meditate, and give yourself to God." He stands at the door of your heart and is still knocking. Open that door, allow the light of His love to enter and allow all your heart's desires to be realized.

When we have achieved a perfect balance between inner peace and outer expression, when we are transformed into living gospels, we will have discovered the most profound meaning of life and of true happiness. A happiness that helps us understand that it is beautiful to love without limits, to have friends, to know people who seek us out to ask for help, comfort and understanding. Help others to climb the mountain and you will already be on the summit.

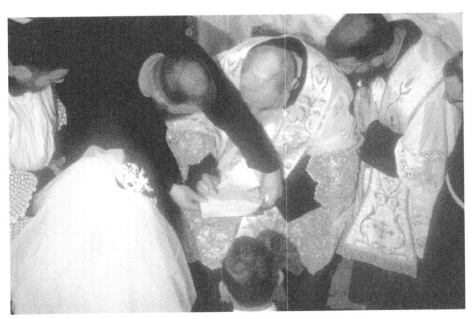

This was the last wedding celebrated by Padre Pio.
Printed with approval of the Archives of the Capuchin Fathers.

153

PADRE PIO: GOD-MAN

In the first part of the book, I wrote that when I was a young man (and unaware of what I was saying), I asked Padre, "Father, does God forgives all sins?" He looked right into my eyes and responded, "Yes, my son. But there is one sin He forgives only with great difficulty: the ingratitude of man from birth to death." Then and there, I accepted his response without thinking much about it. But many years later I understood the importance and significance behind his words, as I will explain shortly. But let's move forward one step at a time.

First, I'll begin with the diary of Lucia Fiorentino, a holy Third Order Franciscan woman. She wrote it under obedience to her spiritual director based on the revelations she was receiving, as recorded in the acts of the process of beatification.

It was 1906 and Jesus Himself in a vision prophesied to her that a priest similar in stature to an enormous tree would come to San Giovanni Rotondo. In 1913, she experienced the vision again when Jesus said, "From far away, a priest symbolized by a large tree will be planted in the friary. That tree will be so great that it will cover the entire world with its shade, and those who shall seek refuge in faith under that tree will find true salvation."

Another document cited by Antonio Socci in his book, "*Il segreto di P. Pio*" ("The Secret of Padre Pio") is that of the mystic, Maria Francesca Foresti, foundress of the Congregation of the Franciscan Sisters of the Adorers [Ita: *Suore Francescane Adoratrici*]. In her diary, she refers to powerful words Jesus said about Padre Pio.

"The soul of Padre Pio is an impregnable fortress"; "He is my refuge in the ingratitude of man"; "He has the same empire as Me, because I, Jesus, live in him"; "He is the masterpiece of My mercy"; "To him I have given all the gifts of My Spirit, as I have given to no other creature"; "He is My perfect imitator, My Host, My altar, My sacrifice, My willingness, My glory."

155

The process of beatification has been opened for Mother Maria Foresti in the city of Bologna.

Let us reflect for a moment on the magnitude of these statements about Padre Pio -- this friar so humble yet so great in the Heart of God. By now, there was little left of Francesco Forgione, because on the human level it was impossible to justify how anyone could live like him with his body crucified alive, unless, as Jesus Himself said, "I, Jesus, live in him." "When Christ appears, we shall be like him, for we shall see him as he is" (1 John 3:2).

Once again, this shows the eternal truth of the gospel -- that Jesus is alive today more than ever. He manifested Himself in the world through the person of Padre Pio making him the source of countless miracles. According to a rough estimate, over 100 million people have come to Padre Pio in San Giovanni Rotondo.

And still today, Jesus continues to reveal Himself daily to cloistered nuns who, in the silence of their cells, pray continuously to stop the wrath of God against this corrupt and degenerate society. He shows Himself in missionaries who have left everything to bring a smile and help abandoned children in Africa and in other parts of the third world. He is present in so many holy priests who carry out their ministries daily. He manifests Himself in us when we comfort the desperate and suffering. He lives in men and women like my dear friend, Giovanni, an industrialist from Venice who every Sunday morning loads his car inconspicuously and anonymously with all kinds of foods to distribute to the poor throughout the city.

Yet due to spiritual blindness and driven by the hectic pace of modern life, people have difficulty seeing the divine light that is within them, that guides them, and that embraces them in God's great mercy. In the wake of so many sins and such ingratitude, Padre Pio wrote to Father Benedetto in 1910:

For some time now, I have felt within me a need, that is, to offer myself to the Lord as a victim for poor sinners and for the souls in Purgatory. This desire has been growing more and more in my heart so that it has become now, I would say, a strong passion. It is true that I have made this offering to the Lord many times, imploring Him to want to pour out on me the punishments that are prepared for sinners and souls in purgatory.

When Padre Pio interceded to obtain a miracle to save some soul which God, in turn, conceded, it was he who offered himself as a sacrificial victim. This was the promise he made in his priestly ordination, "… For You, may I be, in the world, the Way, the Truth, the Life, and for You, a holy priest, a perfect Victim. Padre Pio."

Do you recall the story about the birth of my son, Pio? When I went to thank Padre Pio, while in the presence of Father Giacinto, the Father Provincial, he replied, "You don't have to tell me, I alone know what I did to snatch that child from death."

I recall another episode dating back to 1956. A priest, Fr. Attilio Negrisolo, had asked Padre to pray for a young man from the city of Cattolica who had a brain tumor. It was Easter Vigil and Fr. Attilio sent his greetings to Padre. This was Padre's response, "For me, the days are all equal. Today it seems like a drill is penetrating my head." Then Fr. Attilio asked, "Do you take the evil of all people on yourself?" Padre Pio immediately said, "I wish that were true. Then I would see everyone happy." After he returned to Cattolica, Fr. Attilio discovered that the young man had been miraculously healed.

Jesus accepted the prayer of this beloved son of His by giving him the marks of His crucifixion which literally ripped into the body of this poor little friar. Thus, Jesus showed Himself once again to humanity-- more alive than ever in the body of Padre Pio. As he did with St. Thomas, he revealed His wounds, which have been a source of healing, salvation, consolation and hope.

Cardinal Giuseppe Siri once wrote -- and with good reason, "Padre Pio was the greatest mystic of our century and one of the greatest in the history of the Church."

Padre Pio was the first priest who adhered to the heartfelt invitation of Pope Pius X to offer himself as a victim for sinners, and to seek to prevent the impending disaster of World War I which was about to be unleashed on Europe. Padre had a deep admiration for and devotion to the Pope so much as to take his religious name from him [Tr.: Pio is Italian for Pius]. And that same Pope would die offering himself as victim to the Lord for the world war and for many sinners. These were the ideals which Padre Pio set out to pursue when he embraced his priesthood.

I find it amazing what transpired between St. Luigi Orione and Pope Pius

XI. Fr. Orione once saw Padre Pio praying on his knees before the tomb of Pope Pius X in St. Peter's in Rome. (Of course, he was in bilocation, as Padre Pio never left his cell in San Giovanni Rotondo.) After hearing what Fr. Orione said and knowing of his deep religious sentiment and sound mind, the Pontiff replied, "If you say this, I must believe it."

Only by reading the letters of Padre Pio which cover his extensive correspondence with his spiritual director, Father Agostino, especially between 1911-1913 can we see how God was molding this young friar and uniting him to Himself making him into a: GOD-MAN. He wrote the following to Father Agostino in 1911, "I feel very weak in body and soul, my spiritual father, but I surrender to God. If this be God's will, I wish to suffer ever more to give Him satisfaction."

In the same year, 1911, when Padre Pio was staying in the friary in Venafro in the province of Isernia in the region of Molise, Jesus appeared to him completely wounded with a sword in hand, as a sign of God's wrath. Padre Pio said to him, "My Jesus, how come this morning You are so wounded, Your wounds are so awful today? My Jesus, forgive and lower that sword. If it is to fall, You will find only my head. Yes, I wish to be the victim."

In 1912, he wrote:

Jesus loved me, He wished to place me before so many creatures [i.e. souls]. And when I ask Him what I did to deserve so many consolations, He smiles at me and repeats that nothing is denied to such an intercessor. He asks me only for LOVE in return. But don't I owe Him this perhaps out of gratitude? He so infatuates my heart that He makes me burn totally with His divine fire, the fire of His love. What is this fire that covers me completely? My Father, if Jesus makes us this happy on earth, what will it be like in Heaven?

On February 13, 1913, Padre Pio wrote,

Jesus told me in a vision, "Fear not, I will make you suffer, but I will give you strength. I desire that your soul be purified and tried with daily, hidden martyrdom. Do not be frightened if I allow the devil to torment you, the world to be sickened by you and your loved ones to afflict you.

158

Because nothing will prevail against those who groan under the cross because of My love and I have endeavored to protect them."

Padre Pio was, by now, ready to become a victim for a sinful humanity, a beacon of hope for the suffering.

Then, on March 12, 1913 Padre Pio described to his spiritual director a vision that was as prophetic as well as shocking about human ingratitude.

Jesus told me, "See how My love is repaid by man with such ingratitude! I would have been less offended by them if I had loved them less. My Father no longer wishes to bear them. My Heart has been forgotten; no one cares for My love any longer. My House has become as a theater for many... Even my ministers -- whom I have always regarded with fondness and whom I have loved as the apple of My eye -- should comfort My Heart that is full of bitterness; they should help Me in the redemption of souls. Instead, who would believe that I must receive ingratitude and non-recognition from them? I see, my son, so many of them who, under hypocritical guise, betray Me with sacrilegious communions.

On the following April 7th, Padre wrote:

I saw Jesus who showed me a great crowd of priests and dignitaries of the Church. Jesus turned His horrified gaze away from those priests, as if tired of watching. Then, looking into my eyes, I observed with horror two tears running down His cheeks. He then walked away from that crowd of priests with a great expression of disgust on His face shouting, "BUTCHERS!" Then, turning to me, He said, "My son, do not believe that my agony lasted only three hours. No. On account of the souls who benefited more from Me, I will be in agony until the end of the world. During My agony, my son, one should not sleep. My soul does not go around looking for a drop of human pity [i.e. sympathy], but alas, they leave Me alone under the weight of indifference. My ministers' ingratitude and sleep make My agony even more difficult. What troubles Me the most is that these people add disbelief to their indifference. How many times I would have been there to strike them down had I not been held back by the angels and those loving souls. Write to your [spiritual] father and tell him what you saw and heard this morning. Tell him to show your letter to Father Provincial."

All this had already been prophesied by Jesus when he said, "It is inevitable that scandals come, but woe to anyone through whom they come. It would be better for them to be thrown into the sea with a millstone tied around their neck ... So watch yourselves. If your brother or sister sins against you, rebuke them; and if they repent, forgive them" (Luke 17:1-3). Forgiveness is a word so great that today few people even use it any longer.

Today the situation is worse because that lightning rod by the name of Padre Pio is gone, that giant tree under which we could have found refuge to receive love and divine forgiveness. But above all the situation is worse due to our fault in that we have not professed our faith consistently, as Padre Pio said when he accepted me as his spiritual son, "Be a living gospel."

Today people pray little and badly -- if they pray at all. And this, despite our Heavenly Mother who continually invites us to pray, pray, pray in so many apparitions that still take place today around the world including Medjugorje. Yet, numbly, we often pray out of established habit with our lips and not with the heart.

If we would only recall Paul's letter to the Hebrews, then we would put all our hopes in the immense love of God who is ready to forgive us when He sees our sincere repentance. But this can only take place if we speak the same language of God, "PRAYER," accompanied by deep faith. And this is the faith which Jesus recalls in the Gospel of Luke, "If you had faith like a grain of mustard seed, you could say to this mulberry tree, 'Be uprooted and planted in the sea,' and it would obey you" (17:6).

There are no comments to make inasmuch as the words written by Padre Pio speak for themselves; what more could be added? I cannot even imagine how much pain this vision caused in Padre Pio's heart which he describes in great detail. Think how this poor friar suffered who yearned in love for his beloved Jesus.

What I have just written comes from a collection of letters by Padre Pio which were published in 1987. Formerly, it had been kept confidential within the archive of the Provincial Curia of the Capuchins. I never knew that such a collection of letters of such importance existed. And naively, in 1958, I turned to Padre and asked him, "Father, does God forgive everything?" His response, "Yes! My son, God forgives everything. But there is one sin He has difficulty forgiving: the ingratitude of man from birth to death." Then, after a pause, he added -- giving me a glimmer of hope, "But He knows how to wait."

I never knew that prior to my question, he had experienced a series of visions of Jesus, including the apocalyptic one on March 12, 1913, in which Jesus revealed Himself disgusted and saddened by human ingratitude. Today, with so many scandals that have taken place within the Church, we note with bitterness how prophetic those visions were. In fact, Jesus Himself recommended that Padre Pio speak of them to his spiritual director as well as to the Minister Provincial.

In the silent seclusion of his cell, Padre Pio was mindful of what Jesus said to him on February 13, 1913, "I desire that your soul be purified and tested with daily, hidden martyrdoms." He was faithful to his promise to Jesus; he suffered in silence, and the only person he spoke to was his spiritual director.

St. Teresa of Avila defined prayer as "an intimate conversation of love externalized, without ever tiring, in silence and solitude with the One by whom the soul knows it is loved." To pray is to expose one's soul to the rays of the sun to be warmed and illuminated by Him.

It is clear now that Padre Pio's request was accepted. By now, he had been molded and readied to offer himself as a sacrificial lamb for sinners. And what better imprimatur, though he never wanted them, than the wounds on his body of the signs of the redemption of the eighth day. There, freed from the constraints of time and space, he would become pure light in the Heart of God, a treasure of indescribable beauty in the Kingdom of Heaven. This was the fulfillment of God's plan: "Padre Pio: GOD-MAN."

Now we have the certainty that after 2,000 years, Jesus returned among us in Padre Pio. [Through Padre Pio], He manifests Himself in all His splendor, with all His omnipotence and light that attracts everything to redeem souls to bring them within the Heart of God. Through the intercession of Padre Pio, Jesus desires to be sought through faith and manifested in love.

Daily gratitude to God is the key to obtaining miracles, even when they do not occur. Padre invites us to always be grateful to God for His great goodness, to desire to love Christ -- especially in the poor -- to be available at the feet of Jesus to show Him our love by the example of our lives. And it is that Jesus who is continuously knocking at the door of our hearts; yet we, who listen little, do not open up. Instead, do as St. John Paul II once said, "Open the doors to Christ." Become aware that He is close to us, He is with us and He is in us.

When we realize that God is in our hearts and is close to us each moment of the day, and when we allow Him to direct our every word and thought, then we will become aware of a mysterious strength that comes to us from the Holy Spirit. This strength will show itself and manifest love and brotherhood to all those we come into contact with, who, in turn, will be attracted to this new vision of life.

Then, mystically, we will enter into contact with the mind of God which will enable us to see clearly and consciously manifest all the divine potential that lies within us. Then the voice of the divine Spirit whispers to our heart, "Be calm and entrust yourself to Me with absolute faith. You will find Me always in your heart when you have calm and inner peace. And you will be so full of joy and will talk to Me, serve Me and worship Me that nothing will be more important to you than to hear and feel the rustling of My tender love wherever you go and in whatever you do."

Through the example of his life, Padre Pio desires that we turn to Jesus as a friend with whom we want to share our lives; as the Savior who wishes to purify our souls from selfishness; as the God who aspires to take us up to Himself waiting to greet us in the fullness of the light of eternity. When we are aware that our soul is filled with divine love, infused by the Holy Spirit that came to us through baptism with which we have been clothed in Christ, our life will take on completely new meaning.

That same Holy Spirit will take on life and become a spirit of healing. The spirit will be light that guides our life and a spirit of wisdom, love, and a direct channel to arrive at the Heart of God. Then, thanks to the immense goodness of God who presented Himself to us through Padre Pio with his suffering borne stoically and with regal dignity, we will become a wonderful expression of life.

I would like to leave you with a message of hope in the following words that Padre Pio wrote to his spiritual son, Giovanni Bardazzi. He said, "You must tell everyone that after death I will be more alive than ever. And it will cost me nothing to respond to all those who come asking. No one who shall climb this mountain will come back empty-handed."

Through this book, I have sought to give back a little of what I have received, and this is what this unworthy spiritual son of Padre Pio -- who received so much -- feels he should convey to you.

Dear friends, if the words you have read here touched your heart, then it was not I who have spoken, but the Spirit of God who entered within you.

And here I end, but not before embracing you with a limitless affection, with an intensity of boundless love and with the words Padre Pio said to me:

"MY SON, GIVE THE LOVE WHICH I HAVE PUT IN YOUR HEART TO ALL THOSE TO WHOM YOU DRAW NEAR. IN THIS IS THE MEANING OF LIFE."

Further Reflections from a Spiritual Son

The following chapters are the most recent stories added by Adolfo Affatato. This section was added just prior to the book being published in English.

ENRICO MEDI

Over the years, I observed many well-known people meet with Padre Pio including renowned celebrities.

One particularly distinguished gentleman who was quite close to Padre Pio was a professor named Enrico Medi. Medi was one of the greatest Italian scientists of that era, and I knew him personally as I had the occasion to speak with different times.

I remember him as a poignant man. He was as great as he was humble. After his first meeting with Padre Pio, his life was changed radically. He, too, was awestruck and from that moment onward and had a long relationship with Padre Pio. He frequented San Giovanni Rotondo often.

Like everyone else, when he went to the church of San Giovanni Rotondo for Mass, he waited for the door to open at 4:30 AM. When Prof. Medi served at Padre's Mass it was quite a moving sight to watch him kneeling with his hands folded throughout the entire liturgy. He was like a pillar of salt in prayerful silence and full of emotion.

Medi once said of Padre Pio's Mass:

Participating in Padre Pio's Mass was physically re-living the entire agony of Gethsemane, Calvary, the crucifixion and death. When we assisted at Padre's Mass, we could see the concern of a soul who, on the one hand, was quite afflicted with suffering, and on the other did not want his intense pain extended to his brothers near him. And, like the Lord, he was constantly quivering in pain.

> Participating in Padre Pio's Mass was physically re-living the entire agony at Gethsemane...And, like the Lord, he was constantly quivering in pain.

I can confirm, dear friends, that I, too, had the great privilege of serving at Padre's Mass and what Medi says is sacrosanct and true. You felt directly involved in suffering and were helpless to intervene. Meanwhile, you participated in Padre's torment who -- with the sacred Host in his hands -- repeated over and over, "Lord, I am not worthy" all the while crying.

In an intimate conversation with this beloved [spiritual] son of his, Padre Pio himself once spoke to Medi about what happened at the moment of the consecration. He said, "Enrico, you must understand what it means each day to see my Father, Jesus, killed... killed."

Another aspect that linked Padre Pio to Medi was the passionate love they both shared for the Virgin Mary. In fact, Medi named all six of his daughters after Mary. Padre Pio called the Virgin Mary his "Mammina mia" while Medi called her his "beautiful lady." Medi wrote the following beautiful words about her:

> The Lord created Mary and she has gathered within her all that is beautiful, great, wonderful, stupendous and harmonious -- everything that could possibly be in the design of a human creature. Let us never despair and let us trust in the Mediatrix of All Graces who can read in God's eyes and who knows how to draw out the most wonderful plan of love and joy.

Even now as I reread these words, I still feel a strong sense of emotion. And how can it be otherwise while in the presence of such depth of thought in which love manifests itself for the heavenly Mother without limits?

Medi wrote of Padre Pio's beautiful qualities when he said: "Padre Pio is the naturalness of the supernatural." Everything Padre Pio said, spoke about, and prophesied was expressed in the simplest and most natural way.

Do you remember when Padre Pio called me by name from among the faithful the first time I ever saw him? Without ever having met me before he said, "Adolfo, come here." I stood there motionless thinking that perhaps he was upset with me. When he called me a second time, I raised my hand saying, "Father, are you speaking to me?" And he promptly said, "Is my name, by chance, Adolfo?" He said it so naturally that it seemed, like we already knew one another.

Professor Medi made other beautiful statements about Padre Pio. He said: "Padre Pio is a work of art of the Holy Spirit. And before such a work of art, one cannot comment, one can only remain purely ecstatic."

Here I would like to add that I believe Padre Pio was the masterpiece of the artwork created by God. Never before had the Lord manifested Himself so clearly [as he did] for fifty years in the frail and sick body of a son of St. Francis. Before Padre Pio, a priest had never had the marks of the crucifixion imprinted on his body -- the signs of humanity's redemption, signs he carried with such dignity and regal sovereignty. Padre spilled so much blood to redeem sinners, to bring relief to the sick, and become an actor of so many miracles making reason unreasonable!

To witness such amazing experiences, as I did, implies a responsibility on behalf of those who saw and heard in communicating the wonders of God that came to us through Padre Pio. Our life has meaning only to the extent that we learn how to help others and improve their lives. And this can happen only if we are faithful witnesses to the love of God that continues to occur every day in our lives.

People went to Padre Pio asking for a miracle... and they found God. They found happiness. There was so much happiness when people were around Padre. Let us always remember that happiness is a moment of eternity, an oscillation of the soul in the symphony of the universe.

One evening after the evening service of the exposition of the Blessed Sacrament, I was with the usual small group of spiritual sons waiting near Padre's sitting room to extend our final evening farewells and ask for counsel before he retired to his cell. Prof. Medi happened to be seated next to me that evening. When Padre Pio passed by, everyone kissed his hand. Yet, Medi knelt and bowed his head. Father Carmelo turned to Medi and said, "Professor, why do you, who are so intimate with Padre, lower your head?" And he responded: "Because I am not worthy to look at the face of Christ."

How true were his words! To see him coming toward us dragging his feet -- those pierced feet which he shuffled along from early dawn and carried his body signed with fire by the signs of the crucifixion. How much pain, how much tenderness Padre caused me to feel that evening.

Moreover, it was Jesus Himself who predicted to Padre Pio in a vision, "My son, you shall know love in pain, you shall feel it sharply in the spirit and more sharply still in the body."

I believe that humanity has not yet understood the mission of Padre Pio in all its entirety and magnitude. Only now are we beginning to have a clearer framework by reading his letters and hearing the many testimonies of those who met with him and his spiritual children, including first of all Prof. Enrico Medi.

If, as Antonio Socci wrote in his great work, *The Secret of Padre Pio*, Padre was an "*Alter Christus*," we should consider the words of George Bernanos: "There will come a day in which men cannot pronounce the name of Jesus without weeping."

Yet, the most striking event regarding Prof. Enrico Medi took place one evening. After greeting Padre, we stayed around in the churchyard speaking about God with some other spiritual children including the unforgettable presence of Mario Frisotti, another great spiritual son, who was also very attached to Padre. It was in the 1960s, and I was quite young, but well-pruned and fairly intrepid.

In the presence of this monumental man of culture and faith, I asked a question about God. The professor replied kindly and charitably, "God is the energy that sustains the entire universe, an energy governed by the law of love. Where there is life, there is God. We must enter within ourselves in silence so that this energy of love may nourish our breath and sustain our body." After so many years I still remember his profound words that struck me and left me speechless. Over the years, I have had plenty of time to process and reflect on what I heard that night. How true were his words!

Let us think about humanity for a moment. In the name of the law of love, God created man in His image and likeness. Do you know that a person's heart beats roughly sixty times per minute? That amounts to 3,600 times per hour and 86,400 times a day. The same heart pumps roughly 343 liters of blood in one hour; 8,232 liters a day and about three million liters in one year. Further, there are about 100 billion cells in the human brain and 10 quadrillion in the body.

So why am I giving you the data? So that you may reflect with me for a moment on the wonderful creation that God has made. Do you think there is some long-lasting battery that powers all these cells in unison? Of course not. However, there is an energy underlying them that is never exhausted. And this energy is Divinity. When our earthly sojourn ends, that energy stops beating and with it our earthly life ceases.

We people are a mere particle of that immense divine light, a ray of his divinity. We must realize this and nourish our spirit with inner silence. We will be judged based on the love we have been able to give and on the good we have been able to do.

Padre Pio said so many times that the following conditions are necessary when talking with God: "Silence, meditation, and prayer." God's voice is so sweet and subtle that it can be heard only in the absolute silence of our hearts. Let us banish from within that whirlwind that envelops us each day and causes us to worry about tomorrow.

In a speech entitled, "Science and faith," Medi once said: "Science, by nature, is Christian: that is, searching for the truth, which is a careful investigation of what the will of God is that expresses itself in the natural order (science) and in the supernatural order (faith and theology)."

With great joy I recently learned that in 2013 the diocesan phase of the beatification process of Prof. Medi was completed in the cathedral of Senigallia [in the region of the Marches]. In his keynote speech, Bishop Orlandini underlined that Medi was a wonderful example of Christianity and an authentic witness of evangelical values.

Medi knew how to unite faith and science as a single entity and demonstrated that they lead to only one truth of a God who guides the lives of His creatures with wisdom and infinite love. With his parting words about Padre Pio the day he died, Medi made 100,000 people weep who were assembled in the churchyard. And I sat behind him. What a privilege it was for me!

Medi deserves to be honored as a saint. He was a man who was able to represent his status as a spiritual son of Padre Pio to the utmost. He was also a scientist, a father and an exemplary husband. He had boundless faith, great humility, and an amazing degree of culture. He was a wonderful speaker who touched all those who had the opportunity to listen to him.

From scientist, to spiritual man, to poet: every concept expressed by Enrico Medi always returned to the universality of his concept of faith in a God who is present in each of his creations as man when he says, "Man becomes great when, in his smallness, he gathers the greatness of heaven and the splendor of the earth, and offers them in adoration and love to the heavenly Father."

I cannot conclude this chapter on Enrico Medi without quoting a passage from Letter to a Child in which, once again, this giant of culture and spirituality emerges formed in the school of his great master: Padre Pio.

> Know, my child, that your smiling eye is worth more than all the powerful galaxies. Your smile a star does not have. Antares cannot smile, Andromeda cannot cry. You look at the stars, but the stars do not see you. You are bigger than the stars.

Dear friend who is reading my book, if, while looking up at the sky, you notice a star shining more brightly than the others, stop and send up a message of love. Its name is Enrico Medi, one of the most beautiful and splendid stars of the firmament of heaven, now in the Heart of God and in the arms of his beloved Padre Pio.

THE MIRACULOUS MEDAL - REVISITED

The following story is truly incredible. It is an everyday demonstration that when you were close to Padre Pio, the incredible became credible. The beauty that we were so accustomed to happening around us began to seem quite normal. However, this is still true and he still acts with the same naturalness today after many years. In fact, Padre Pio -- who is now divine light and is at one with God the Father -- acts as if he were still alive here on earth. He is the priest who once said, "I will make more noise from heaven than when I was alive on earth." I am reminded of the words of St. Peter: "Beloved, with the Lord one day is like a thousand years and a thousand years are like one day. The Lord does not delay his promise, as some regard delay, but he is patient with you, not wishing that any should perish" (2 Pet 3:8-9).

Now let's return to the events at hand. Do you remember the episode I wrote about in the first edition of my book? We spiritual sons were in the sitting room next to Padre's cell one evening when Padre Pio needed his handkerchief. Father Lino asked me to go and get it from the bedside table in Padre's cell. I did so with great joy. When I went in and retrieved the handkerchief, I noticed a number of miraculous medals of the Virgin Mary which Padre used to give to sick people and children.

I was tempted to take one, but I stopped thinking to myself, "If Padre Pio realizes it, what kind of impression would I be making?" In fact, when I returned and to Padre handed him the handkerchief, he said to me, "So it takes that long to get a handkerchief?" Then, he added in the soft voice of a father scolding his son, "And thank goodness you put that medal back, because I don't speak with *mariuli* [Tr.: dialect for 'thieves']."

I'll let you imagine what I went through in that moment. Once again I was amazed -- as was everyone else present. Of course I had to apologize and explain everything to Father Lino who said, "Adolfo, don't you know that you can't hide anything from Padre Pio?"

Nonetheless, I went away that night somewhat disappointed that I did not get the medal of the Virgin Mary. I was certainly aware that the Lord had already gifted me with so many other relics of Padre, which I jealously guard. Yet, that medal remained in my heart.

So, now let's fast forward to June, 2012, exactly fifty-two years later. I was in Rome with my wife visiting our daughter, Maria Grazia, who lives there. I went to the church of San Gioacchino, near her house on Via Gracchi, where there is a beautiful chapel for Perpetual Adoration. I spent some time praying the rosary and meditating for a little while, and then I left.

While opening the door to leave, I distinctly heard the voice of Padre Pio say to me, "Go back." In that moment for one reason or another, I didn't pay much attention to what I heard and I kept walking. Yet, I heard the same voice say again, "Go back." So, both as an act of faith (as well as curiosity), I went back to the same bench where I had just been sitting to recite the rosary. I knelt down again and, to my amazement, on the counter in front of me I discovered a miraculous medal of the Virgin Mary!

You can imagine how much joy and emotion I felt in that moment. fifty-two years later, Padre Pio decided to delight me. How much love I felt from Padre! How will I ever be able to give back this divine love that constantly surprises... the love that Padre showed me and still shows me even today?

More and more, I still feel the prophetic words he said to me that night when he asked me to accompany him to his cell after confessions. He told me: "My son, I will help you and I will support you in body and mind until the last moment of your life."

> "My son, I will help you and I will support you in body and mind until the last moment of your life."

But why me, Lord? I have asked myself this question many times, and as usual I find the answer in the Scriptures. First of all, there is John, the Apostle of love, whom I love the most. He was the one who rested on Jesus' chest and he is the Disciple whom Jesus loved. He wrote:

As the Father loves me, so I also love you... I no longer call you slaves, because a slave does not know what his master is doing. I have called you friends, because I have told you everything I have heard from my Father. It was not you who chose me, but I who chose you and appointed you to go and bear fruit that will remain, so that whatever you ask the Father in my name he may give you. (John 15:9; 15-16)

Even the question which St. Jude of Thaddeus posed to the Lord, "Lord, why do you have so much love for me?" finds a response in this passage from the Gospel of John.

Returning to my humble situation, I can tell you that after a number of years of frequently visiting Padre, I, too, posed the same question to Fr. Lino Barbati, a great soul and great friend. I asked him, "But Father Lino, why did Padre Pio choose me?" A few months later, he gave me my answer, "Padre Pio once told me, 'Because there is something good in that young man.'" With his gift of reading hearts, in his infinite mercy, the Lord showed Padre Pio that there was potential in me leading him to accept me as one of the elite of his spiritual children. What a great honor, what infinite joy! Consider that it was difficult to receive absolution from Padre at the end of confession let alone be accepted as his spiritual son. It was a great commitment and a huge responsibility in the midst of a very strict school.

Padre used to always say to his children, "In the confessional, I am a judge. Outside, I am a loving and caring father toward all his children, but especially to those who need help." Padre Pio was an uncomfortable priest of an uncomfortable Church. For Padre, even a small lie represented an offense and a sin against divine love.

So returning to the question, "Why me?" I cannot answer without considering, once again, the Gospel of St. John. Padre's spiritual children -- and all those who visited him for that matter -- were filled with many graces through Padre's love to the point that he said, "I will remain at the gates of heaven, until the last of my spiritual children enters."

Padre Pio once called Dr. Sanguinetti from Tuscany entrusting him to administer his beloved creation, the House for the Relief of Suffering. His response was, "Father, but I do not believe that I am the right person...Why are you calling me?" And Padre promptly responded, "It's not important that you believe, because God believes in you." Amazing!!!

Let's not forget other great spiritual sons of Padre whom I had the occasion to meet: Carlo Campanini, Professor Gerardo de Caro, Professor Francesco Lotti.

In fact, I had an intimate friendship with the latter. The story of his life written by his son, Father Luciano Lotti, is very moving. I spoke to him personally about many stories [written in the book], which for me [reading it] was like re-living the fifteen years when I was close to Padre. And what about Countess Telfner who said to Padre Pio one day: "Father, I am grateful to my husband who introduced me to you." And Padre -- with his usual angelic candor using words that were completely spiritual -- said, "But I've known you since you were born and have been following you since then."

Do you remember what I said when I told him I loved him? He said: "My child, but you do not know the love that I have for you." This was true not only for me but for all those who placed themselves under his spiritual guidance. Padre loved everyone without distinction. So many people had many encounters with him that strongly influenced their personal lives.

A LIVE MIRACLE

I received many e-mails after the first edition of my book came out, including from some wonderful people who testified to having found their faith through Padre Pio. And this is beautiful, because I feel the purpose of my testimony being fulfilled in it: bringing souls to God.

I still hear Padre saying to me and to all his spiritual children: "My children, you are part of me, you fill me with joy because you have understood my mission on earth. Do not stop, but continue bearing witness to my teachings. Your task is to bring souls to God. Sow and I will deal with watering the seeds of your testimony so that they become flowers shining in the heavenly homeland."

Thus, Padre did not want "admirers" but rather "imitators" of his love and suffering for Jesus Christ -- first among which were the many misunderstandings, envy, and malice which he was victim of throughout his entire life. But, like a little lamb, he never resisted. Never did words of revenge emerge from his mouth; instead, there was always and only love and forgiveness.

One of the most touching e-mails I received dealt with a miracle I experienced unfolding as if it were live. It was from a woman named Eleanora and I have printed it here in full.

December 16, 2011 at 2:25 pm:
Let me begin by saying thank you immensely. I just finished reading your wonderful and touching book. I am a wife, having been married for three years, and I have always had an infinite devotion to our beloved Padre Pio… I feel immense tenderness and infinite sweetness for him, and just thinking about him moves me.
You know, Mr. Affatato, I pray to him so much. But lately I pray even

more so that he will intercede for us and make us more deserving of the most miraculous gift of the Lord -- the arrival of a little baby to love -- that we have been waiting for a while now. What gives me strength and optimism day after day is faith -- a strength I did not believe that I had. And often I speak with Padre Pio with my heart asking him to make this miracle arrive. I cry in front of a picture of him during times of distress. Reading your book was like a ray of sunshine. It gave me even more hope and more optimism. Every single word was a continuous message like: "Pray with your heart and God will listen to you."

You know, the very thought that you were close to "my" beloved Padre excites me immensely. Just thinking that you spoke to him, touched him, and enjoyed his light -- how wonderful all this is.

And this is why I am humbly asking you to speak to Padre Pio about this little miracle of pregnancy. I ask him with my heart in my hand and with so much trust that you will do this with the hope that our love will nourish a tiny little miracle whom we will then love so much!

Whenever I'm at the tomb of Padre Pio in San Giovanni Rotondo, I invariably cry. I cry. I cry and I say this so that you will know how loyal I am to the man who spent his life in a way so full of suffering and so full of love. A man of many emotions.

Thank you for your willingness. I thank you for the wonderful gift of your book.

My aunt who attended a conference you gave in Crecchio gave it to me saying, "Read it, it's incredible." And it truly was, so I got two more. Thank you, thank you, thank you.

Looking forward to your response, I cordially send my greetings. Eleonora

Dear friends who are reading my book, especially those of you who may not know Padre Pio, it is my wish -- with all my heart -- to create a true picture of who Padre really is. And this is coming from one who saw and heard.

Padre Pio is the one who tells us: "My children, learn, love, forgive, suffer, offer, pray, strive so that your life is imbued by the example of Christ, to the point that your hearts are established with his and they beat in unison." The heart of Padre Pio, even if pierced, was so great as to embrace the sufferings and pains of mankind.

In his earthly mission, Padre Pio represents something sublime and divinely attractive that throws us into the arms of Christ. So then all the adjectives used to describe him have only one objective -- that of considering his presence in our lives: Christocentric. And generating Christ in those who desired to live in Him.

His Christocentric action is everywhere, and it germinates the Savior. This means that it tends to produce in us a union that is ever more profound, complete, and personal with Jesus. And this is so that the light of the Word of God invades us and pervades us completely.

Padre Pio is like a translucent sacrament that makes the luminous divine presence radiate within us. He makes our being much more present in God and much more interior to the life of Jesus -- inasmuch as we are united as children to Our Lady through the rosary.

After receiving Ms. Eleonora's email, I wrote the following response to her:

Dear Eleanora, it would be too little to say that I am merely happy. Yet again Padre Pio has shown how much he loves us, which I have never had any doubts. Let us give glory to God for helping us know His will through the intercession of Padre Pio. Thank you, good Father for everything you have given us. And with prayerful hearts full of love and gratitude, we join ourselves to Mary Most Holy, saying: "My soul magnifies the Lord, my spirit rejoices in God my Savior." A big hug, Adolfo.

Finally, I received confirmation of the miracle in this email received on May 7, 2014:

Hello Mr. Adolfo, I am writing to tell you that on February 10, I became a mother!!!
I prayed to my Padre Pio, who surely made it happen. We named our daughter Aurora, and she is a darling. We had her baptized in a beautiful and moving ceremony. Then, with our minds full of gratitude I turned to Padre immediately after Mass, and I went to the front of a statue of Padre Pio in the church and left a bouquet of flowers to thank him.

Now I feel a strong desire to get down to San Giovanni Rotondo to have my baby blessed. And I would like you to help me -- to talk with the friars and tell them that my prayers were answered, and thank that wonderful friar whom I love, because I feel the need to shout out my thanks. I hope you can help me out.

I am so happy, Mr. Adolfo, and believe me, I have a joy in my heart that you cannot imagine combined with the awareness of not being alone. I have a special friend who enlightens me every day -- with a white beard, a brown robe, half-gloves, and sandals with his crucified feet.

I gently await your reply. Eleonora

But what reply could I give? It was Padre Pio himself who said to me one day, as I already wrote in another chapter: "My son, there where God is, reason has no more reason to exist." It is clear that in this case there was evidence of God's intervention. But the answer was given by Ms. Eleanora when she wrote, "I pray with much love."

So how could the miracle of this new creature not come about when confronted with these petitions through the intercession of Padre Pio, to whom God cannot deny anything? It would have been a contradiction of the words of Jesus Himself when He said, "Ask and it will be given to you; seek and you will find; knock and the door will be opened to you." And it would also be a contradiction of the words Padre Pio wrote to Giovanni Bardazzi, "No one shall climb this mountain in vain... no one will be back empty-handed."

What did Ms. Eleanora do? She prayed, she prayed with great faith. And the Lord rewarded her faith by not considering what she desired to be contrary to His divine plans. Because let us always remember: it is faith that leads to the Heart of God.

Yet many ask and do not receive. Why is this? We find an answer in the letter of St. James: "You desire but do not have, so you kill. You covet but you cannot get what you want, so you quarrel and fight. You do not have because you do not ask God. When you ask, you do not receive, because you ask with wrong motives, that you may spend what you get on your pleasures" (James 4:2-3).

We usually ask based on our human desires, and not based on doing the divine will. The better way to achieve what we wish for would be to formulate the request in this way: "Lord, this is my human desire. If it is good and just, bless it and fulfill it. You guide my thoughts, words, and actions in the right direction because, Lord, you know what I do not know, you see what I do not see, you know if what I desire is good and right for me. So, good Father, Thy will be done, the only will that can give peace and serenity."

Padre Pio, with his great love expressed vertically toward God and horizontally toward man, helped us understand in a practical way that when we abandon ourselves into the arms of the Virgin Mary -- which was Padre's fixed reference point for going straight to the Heart of God -- this is not escapism for disappointed people, but rather is the key to understanding and receiving all we need, and it gives meaning to our earthly sojourn. Once this step is accomplished, we will see life from an entirely different angle. And as we continue our journey, everything will be clear and everything will be unveiled in the time established by God. Believe me, I have experienced all this in my own life.

According to the teaching of Padre Pio, we must place nothing before the love of Christ. God has no use for our acts of worship if we do not follow through with authentic witness of faith in our daily life by loving and respecting others. When we offer someone a smile and a kind word, then we will be as the light which scatters the darkness of life or the water that quenches the desert of human life.

I must confess that I am often struck by the evil that is around us. But I am also comforted by all the goodness that grows in silence around us. And this goodness includes the prayers of the many good souls, including Ms. Eleanora's, which every night -- in the silence of their homes -- rise up toward the Most High. And in this a coherent and responsive attitude follows their inner belief.

Padre Pio saw the continual repetition of prayer like a sweet musical strength and consolation coming down more and more into souls who yearned for the love of God. His sweet tears were incessant springs of grace that flowed down on all those who came to him.

The true Christian, as molded by Padre Pio, is the one who knows how to be nourished by the Word of God. And when you live in this common purpose, all life experiences as revealed through the guidance of Padre, bring one deep into the meaning of earthly existence. And in this context, in serenity of the body and for after Mass, and I went to the front of a statue of Padre Pio in the church and left a bouquet of flowers to thank him.

Now I feel a strong desire to get down to San Giovanni Rotondo to have my baby blessed. And I would like you to help me -- to talk with the friars and tell them that my prayers were answered, and thank that wonderful friar whom I love, because I feel the need to shout out my thanks. I hope you can help me out.

I am so happy, Mr. Adolfo, and believe me, I have a joy in my heart that you cannot imagine combined with the awareness of not being alone. I have a special friend who enlightens me every day -- with a white beard, a brown robe, half-gloves, and sandals with his crucified feet.

I gently await your reply. Eleonora

But what reply could I give? It was Padre Pio himself who said to me one day, as I already wrote in another chapter: "My son, there where God is, reason has no more reason to exist." It is clear that in this case there was evidence of God's intervention. But the answer was given by Ms. Eleanora when she wrote, "I pray with much love."

So how could the miracle of this new creature not come about when confronted with these petitions through the intercession of Padre Pio, to whom God cannot deny anything? It would have been a contradiction of the words of Jesus Himself when He said, "Ask and it will be given to you; seek and you will find; knock and the door will be opened to you." And it would also be a contradiction of the words Padre Pio wrote to Giovanni Bardazzi, "No one shall climb this mountain in vain... no one will be back empty-handed."

What did Ms. Eleanora do? She prayed, she prayed with great faith. And the Lord rewarded her faith by not considering what she desired to be contrary to His divine plans. Because let us always remember: it is faith that leads to the Heart of God.

Yet many ask and do not receive. Why is this? We find an answer in the letter of St. James: "You desire but do not have, so you kill. You covet but you cannot get what you want, so you quarrel and fight. You do not have because you do not ask God. When you ask, you do not receive, because you ask with wrong motives, that you may spend what you get on your pleasures" (James 4:2-3).

We usually ask based on our human desires, and not based on doing the divine will. The better way to achieve what we wish for would be to formulate the request in this way: "Lord, this is my human desire. If it is good and just, bless it and fulfill it. You guide my thoughts, words, and actions in the right direction because, Lord, you know what I do not know, you see what I do not see, you know if what I desire is good and right for me. So, good Father, Thy will be done, the only will that can give peace and serenity."

Padre Pio, with his great love expressed vertically toward God and horizontally toward man, helped us understand in a practical way that when we abandon ourselves into the arms of the Virgin Mary -- which was Padre's fixed reference point for going straight to the Heart of God -- this is not escapism for disappointed people, but rather is the key to understanding and receiving all we need, and it gives meaning to our earthly sojourn. Once this step is accomplished, we will see life from an entirely different angle. And as we continue our journey, everything will be clear and everything will be unveiled in the time established by God. Believe me, I have experienced all this in my own life.

According to the teaching of Padre Pio, we must place nothing before the love of Christ. God has no use for our acts of worship if we do not follow through with authentic witness of faith in our daily life by loving and respecting others. When we offer someone a smile and a kind word, then we will be as the light which scatters the darkness of life or the water that quenches the desert of human life.

I must confess that I am often struck by the evil that is around us. But I am also comforted by all the goodness that grows in silence around us. And this goodness includes the prayers of the many good souls, including Ms. Eleanora's, which every night -- in the silence of their homes -- rise up toward the Most High. And in this a coherent and responsive attitude follows their inner belief.

Padre Pio saw the continual repetition of prayer like a sweet musical strength and consolation coming down more and more into souls who yearned for the love of God. His sweet tears were incessant springs of grace that flowed down on all those who came to him.

The true Christian, as molded by Padre Pio, is the one who knows how to be nourished by the Word of God. And when you live in this common purpose, all life experiences as revealed through the guidance of Padre, bring one deep into the meaning of earthly existence. And in this context, in serenity of the body and spirit, through the intercession of Padre Pio, God will always give us what we ask when it is for our own good, as seen from a spiritual and eternal vantage point as happened to Ms. Eleanora.

I would like to extend the same wish to this new little child that Padre Pio offered my son, Pio, when I brought him to him for a blessing after the events of his birth: "May she be good, holy, and live to be very old."

SILENCE, MEDITATION AND PRAYER

After many years, all the words, answers, and thoughts I received from Padre Pio during my fifteen years visiting him led me to a careful analysis of each episode in which I witnessed or received something. I will now tell you about one of the episodes I remember the best.

After the exposition of the Blessed Sacrament one evening, as was usual custom, Padre Pio was sitting with a few close friends in the parlor next to his cell. We were immersed in absolute silence and were all taking delight in Padre -- who was praying continuously -- when a young friar suddenly asked him a question: "Padre, so why are you not saying anything this evening?" Without putting down his rosary, Padre Pio stopped and looked at him. After pausing for a moment, he said solemnly, "In your opinion, what do you think I'm doing? I'm talking to God." Then, lifting up the rosary, he added, "This is the language of God."

> "In your opinion, what do you think I'm doing? I'm talking to God." Then, lifting up the rosary, he added, "This is the language of God."
> --Padre Pio

There is no way I can express in human words the feelings that pervaded my soul at that moment. I can only say that I felt a great joy as a powerful radiant light emanated from his bright face. This light shone deep down inside me and pierced my heart penetrating every cell of my body. It gave me so much peace, joy, and happiness. It was the light of the Holy Spirit who, with His omniscience, was using Padre Pio as a channel to come to us all who were near him. Everything was beautiful and divine.

Here I would like to recall the words of Socrates who once said, "The wise man does not break silence other than to say something more important than silence." And what could be more important than that moment of complete and total union between Padre Pio and God? All the laws of time and space no longer had meaning because Padre Pio was in God -- he was in Christ through the Holy Spirit who fulfills all things.

In an earlier chapter, I told the story how I once tried to get a glimpse of the stigmata on Padre's hands. And he said, "My son, these are things you cannot understand, because where God is, reason has no more motive to exist." Only now after many years do I understand the importance of what Padre said to me then. To have a relationship with God several things are necessary: Silence, meditation and prayer. In this chapter, I would like to focus on these three points to understand more and better the validity of these words in order to get to the Heart of God.

In his words to the young friar, Padre Pio answered wisely when there really was no suitable answer. He used the right words at the right time in the right form. Because it is only in prayerful and meditative silence in which one can listen to the divine words maturing within.

In that moment, the words of Tagore suddenly came to my mind, "Stop for a moment from going about agitated and rushed in your everyday life. Render everything inside you calm. Rest in silence, and you will hear voices never before heard. You will taste the life of a world that was unknown to you before; you will love what you previously despised; you will flee from what you previously sought."

Padre Pio's example once again demonstrates that humanity's true being -- man's spiritual essence -- is oneness with God. We must be aware of God's presence within us, as Saint Paul reminds us. We must open ourselves up to it and become channels allowing all the power of the Holy Spirit to flow within us.

The truth of human life is that every person should come to a full knowledge and awareness of unity with the divine self that is within by opening up to it. Thus, we speak the powerful words that Jesus Hmself taught us: "May Thy will be done." Then, union becomes perfect and the rest will come.

Assuming that God is a good Father -- immensely good -- and He desires for us to be happy already during our sojourn here on earth below, we must do nothing other than abandon ourselves into His arms and allow ourselves to be inundated with His love. We must remember that we are simultaneously creatures and creators of everything we fulfill in our lives. In fact, everything we achieve is the result of our thoughts taking shape in the manner willed by us.

People were created with free will. Therefore, by freeing our minds from all that is negative (such as anger, bitterness, resentment), and filling it with things that are positive with the aid of the Holy Spirit working in us -- as St. Paul in the letter to the Galatians, "love, joy, peace, patience, kindness, goodness, faithfulness, gentleness, and control over self" (Gal 5:22) -- we discover that the instrument of a creative strength exists in our thoughts rendering nothing impossible. And this strength is the light of the Holy Spirit who takes command of our lives.

On our part, we just have to have much faith in a good Father who is alive and concrete and is always at our side to support us with His strength. Our job is to be witnesses of this immense power that works in us.

Imagine for a moment a large tree with many branches full of monkeys jumping around and swinging from one branch to another at breakneck speed. This is what people's minds are like. Most people live in a constant state of agitation. They are either thinking about the past or worrying about the future. They never live in the present moment.

Here is another beautiful passage from a poem by Tagore: "Yesterday is a dream, tomorrow is a vision; only by living today intensely and serenely can we make the dream golden and the vision full of hope." We must realize that we were created in the image and likeness of God whose presence is within us. When it becomes effective, is a force of unimaginable power. We must free the branches of the tree from our thoughts. In this way, we can soothe our minds and thus make contact with the divine light within us.

We must always remember that God is love! We must become a channel that opens to the creative strength of God, who with His love fills our soul. But how do we achieve this? With absolute silence full of love and gratitude. In this way, we can create an ideal climate to have contact with God. Thus, we will awaken in us the new man, and the result will be the rediscovery of faith in ourselves, calm, peace and unwavering faith that will show us the way.

Do you remember when I asked Padre if God forgives all sins? His response was: "God is a good Father, He forgive everything. But there is a sin that he has difficulty forgiving: the ingratitude of man from birth to death." This statement is confirmed by an apparition of Jesus to Blessed Sister Maria Foresti in which Jesus said: "Padre Pio is my fortress, my refuge from the ingratitude of men, to him I have conferred the powers of the Holy Spirit as to no other creature, because I, Christ, live in him."

Because the same divine spark in Padre Pio is in every creature. But it was Padre Pio who represented the crowning achievement of God's creation, his masterpiece. Yet, we must be convinced that we, too, are worthy of the love of God. In this way, we can open the doors of our hearts so that this love flows increasingly and abundantly.

How many people offer up a thought to God when they get out of bed in the morning and thank Him for everything He has given them? If you don't already do so, you can say the following words: "Lord, my God, at the beginning of this day I consecrate myself and all my things into Your hands. To You I remit all that concerns me so that Your will be done. With your Holy Spirit, keep mastery over my thoughts and feelings, help my intentions, support my actions, take possession of my life."

As with Padre Pio, we, too, must convince ourselves that it is in silence where we enter within ourselves to discover our true identity: "God." In silence, the doors of power that are within open up. The Spirit thinks, it acts, it is life. It is the Creator who is omnipotent and omniscient of all that is within us, and we are in Him. We have only one task: to always remain in the grace of God in order to receive these gifts. Now you can better understand the reflection that the silence of Padre Pio led me to that enchanted evening.

But silence is just the beginning -- it is merely the door that introduces us to meditation. By continually practicing silence, the body relaxes and leads us to the state of meditation. In this way, we become aware of the fundamental purpose of meditation that is found in the relation at the foundation of our life: relationship with God the Creator. As we move forward in inner relaxation, we become increasingly aware that the origin of the new peace that pervades our everyday life is nothing other than the life of God within us. In order for this to happen, however, our will needs to participate and desire to be in peace. Thus, the psalmist urges us: "Be still and know that I am God" (Psalm 46:10).

Our redemption, attained by Jesus, has transformed the existence of the human conscience which becomes aware of the love of God poured into our hearts through the Holy Spirit. The Spirit of God in man is everything: knowledge, love, power, life, intelligence and strength that is present in the earthly life of every creature. The moment when we realize that our origin is divine -- that God is our Creator -- we can fulfill our potential.

When we begin practicing meditation, we seek to concentrate and focus our thoughts on the Father, the Son, and the Holy Spirit. Yet, in the end we pursue an immensely greater goal: that of detaching from all things that are fleeting. This, in fact, leads to the ultimate goal: no longer thinking of God, but striving to be in God.

It is one thing to acknowledge that Jesus is the Son of God and He is] the way that leads us to the Heart of God. Yet, it is something else to experience the presence of Jesus and the power of the Holy Spirit within us, and in doing so be drawn into the Heart of God. In the prayerful silence of meditation, a process is begun within us in which we discover who we really are: a divine spark, a ray of His divinity.

This is how we can explain Padre Pio's long silences. He was totally in God. The only obstacle that separated him from God was his frail body which was battered and torn by the signs of the crucifixion. In him there was nothing human left. Everything was light, everything was divine wisdom that came to us even in his deafening silence, as he told us that night, "Silence is the language of God."

In today's society, every moral value is in decline. We are poisoned daily by the press and television with news of crime. Mothers murdering their children, children killing their parents, and public officials who create scandal by their example. It goes from bad to worse. In this context, the only valid point of reference that remains is to take refuge in that giant of holiness: Padre Pio. This is because the lives of great men (in the words of Tagore) teach us: "We can make of our existence something sublime that leaves footprints on the sand that cannot be erased by time."

Padre Pio once said, "I will make more noise from heaven." So many people who are desperate and leveled by pain go to his tomb in search of an answer or a sign to assuage their pain. And there they find peace of mind.

This was all prophesied by Padre Pio in the 1960s when he wrote to Giovanni Bardazzi, his spiritual son, "You must tell everyone that after death I will be more alive than ever. And it will cost me nothing to respond to all those who come asking. No one who shall climb this mountain will come back empty-handed."

Today there is a great shortage of saints, of people who in the silence of prayer are like a lightning rod for this increasingly sinful world, of people like Padre Pio who take sins on themselves and offer themselves as victims for the conversion of sinners. Padre Pio's earthly mission was: "A crucified man who lived on earth for the redemption of sinners and for the relief of suffering humanity."

Saints are born of prayer which is accompanied by the witness of their [holy] lives. And what greater and more illuminated example, unparalleled in the history of the Church, is there than Padre Pio who lived for fifty years with the marks of crucifixion on his body? It's as if the trasverberation [spiritual wounding] of his heart was not enough. He had become a living prayer. Some say, with much credibility, that he prayed fifty complete rosaries every day.

St. Yves said when the Holy Spirit takes command of a human life and permeates his entire body, the Holy Spirit is always in action even during the person's sleep. Padre Pio demonstrates this. One night after Padre Pio had gone to sleep, Father Eusebio tried to take the rosary from his hand to keep as a souvenir. However, he was not able to and it was as if the rosary were stuck between his fingers. Even while asleep, Padre Pio continued to pray because the Holy Spirit within him was always awake. The next morning when he saw Fr. Eusebio, he said, "So what were you trying to do last night? If you wanted a souvenir, all you had to do was ask." Then, he stopped, took the rosary and gave it to him.

Jesus tells us, "Whatever you ask for in faith, you will obtain" [Matthew 21:22]. This shows us that faith is the key to prayer. Here is a practical example of this: if I pick up the telephone and dial someone in America, if I don't speak English, my effort is useless. We will not be able to understand one another if we do not speak the same language.

And so it is with prayer: faith is the essential element of our prayer. But a few minutes are not enough. We cannot consider God like a coin slot where we just have to quickly throw in a Hail Mary without faith to obtain the miracle.

The same happened with Padre Pio. Many approached him asking for his intercession to obtain a miracle, but they did not readily understand that if God had created that encounter [with Padre Pio], it was because people -- with their bodies obscured by sin -- were to begin a journey of inner conversion. And here was Padre Pio's great mission: to stave off and eliminate all that separated people from God. He wanted to make the divine spark within shine once again. With his body and with his stigmata, Padre Pio did not wish to dazzle but to enlighten; he did not seek to impose but to propose. He especially did not want admirers, but rather imitators.

But in order to ask in faith, we need to have intimacy with God and believe that He is not an abstract entity but a living Person comprised of love who is ready to take control of our lives. We should admit our human weakness and ask in humility. With these foundations, there are no limits to our prayer requests we ask in faith. Jesus Himself proves it when He says, "Whatever you ask for in prayer, believe that you have received it, and it will be yours" (Mark 11:24).

Creating this space of intimacy means awaking to the reality of the God who lives within us. If we do not enter into this space, God will always remain far from us. And this is true even if we invoke the intercession of Padre Pio; our relationship remains empty.

Thus, the key to arriving at the Heart of God, with the help of Padre Pio, and accessing this spiritual world around us is: stillness, silence, and time. Jesus tells us to "Let your 'Yes' mean 'Yes,' and your 'No' mean 'No.' Anything more is from the evil one" [Matthew 5:37]. This is why one prays so much better in silence rather than by talking, especially babbling.

Macarius the Great also reminds us, "The very foundation of prayer is serious immersion in reflection."

And now we return to where we started: the silence of Padre Pio. These are the thoughts that were aroused in me when Padre said to the young friar, "Now, I'm talking to God." Each day, in silent and faithful prayer, he entrusted to God his mission that began on the day he took his solemn vows when he said: "For You, may I be, in the world, the Way, the Truth, the Life, and for You, a holy priest, a perfect Victim."

Padre Pio and I

Testimonials

What follows are some emails and testimonials I have received. They are lessons in life, and reflections worth reading. They are from people who were lost but found faith, or who were suffering and found serenity, as well as some relatives of mine who shared their thoughts. From these messages, we can find the yeast to continue along our journey of interior growth.

[Tr.: Some emails and testimonials from the original Italian publication were omitted.]

The first entry is from Adolfo's wife, Franca
Dear Adolfo,
Your testimonies have been and always will be like dew drops for all the people who are thirsting to know, to discover, or to increase their faith.
I am sure that your goal of writing about your beautiful experiences of having lived close to a saint has been reached. I shall never tire of thanking you for all you have given me during all these years spent together. If I only go back 50 years when we met and you did nothing other than talk about this Capuchin saint (I was a little jealous, I must admit, alas jealous of a Saint!) who has always protected us, I see that our life was lived in his light. That light which he placed in you from your youth, throughout your university studies, in your work, in our marriage, during the birth of our children (as you recalled also in the great miracle of Pio), and finally during my illness. I will always be by your side when they call you for conferences (which are still always rousing), and when my face is lined with tears, these are nothing other than Padre's caresses.
Thank you for everything.

Your wife,
Franca

Dear Adolfo,
I would like to thank you for this beautiful gift which, with the deep feeling of friendship that has bound us for many years, you wished to give me.
For me, Padre Pio and I is like a sequel and the compendium of many conversations through which you have allowed me to get to know this wonderful man: Padre Pio.

I clearly remember one of our first meetings. You mentioned Padre Pio and related your personal experiences. That conversation transformed me and set a light within me; a thirst for knowledge of Padre that grew to the point of receiving direct testimony of his greatness.

It has been a dialogue that has continued, as you know, and now I have found many episodes in this book which we talked about. But I have to add that there are additional amounts of involvement: the plain and touching language, especially dense in veneration and stimulating toward the peak which Padre Pio was an exceptional witness in the last century.

Therefore, I wish to thank you from the bottom of my heart for the effort you have made through which many people can derive great spiritual benefit.

This book demonstrates just how your excellent professional business was always accompanied by the witness of God's love for that wonderful intercession of the Holy Friar who continues to manifest to you his goodness, which you deserve.

G.G. from Roma

Dear Adolfo,

I read your book and our friendship won't get in the way of me telling you that I found it very nice, pleasant and interesting.

You were to make your relationship with Padre Pio into a beautiful story, and all the episodes identified therein reveal your deep devotion to the friar whom you met when you were a young student purely out of curiosity. And that from that first meeting he proved to be not merely "one who could read people's minds and predict the future," as your friends said, but, rather "a man who knew how to suffer, a priest who knew how to pray, a Capuchin priest who was a follower of St. Francis whom Divine Providence gave you as a guide in your life."

I appreciated very much -- as they were relevant -- the precious references to the gospel, holy books, the lives of the saints, and especially St. Paul whose letters deserve to be read and meditated upon more.

In my humble opinion, however, the greatest value of the book is how it has been able to identify, from the onset, the basic tenets of the spirituality of Padre Pio, which are, as you were able to discern during your years of closeness to Padre: suffering, prayer, the ministry of confession and the celebration of Holy Mass.

Thank you, dear Adolfo, for giving me, by reading your book, the great joy of staying with Padre Pio even for a little bit, the saint who, as you know, I, too, had the good fortune of meeting on this earth.

I salute you, dear Adolfo and in imitation of the sentence of the disciples of Emmaus, hope for you and for me and Franca and Ermelinda, "Mane Nobis San Pio" [Remain with us, St. Pio].

With affection always.
M.V. from Foggia

Dear Sir,

I read with great interest the book you wrote in which you have assembled wonderful memoirs as a spiritual son of Padre Pio, a qualification which, unfortunately, I do not have.

I firstly admired the proper insistence with which you placed the events and actors of a spiritual life so intensely lived: the actor of each miracle is always and only God; Padre Pio is therefore a wonderful mediator of God on behalf of a humanity all too often inattentive and distracted.

And Padre always noted this relationship of values between humanity and God, to which he dedicated the entire wonderful charge of his human sufferings.

And hence it was from here whereby his apparent abruptness arose with which he sometimes moved among uncontrollable crowds who placed their miraculous hopes in Padre Pio himself, subjecting him to veritable assaults toward his person just to touch his habit or other such religionist behavior that he did not accept. Therefore, it was just that "he did not admit them!"

We physicians at the hospital of Relief of Suffering had the fortune -- when the weather was nice and our commitments less pressing -- to be able to be close to him in the early afternoon in his sitting room or in the garden and to enjoy some time with him. And during such times of infrequent rest during his day, Padre Pio was often cheerful and even funny as he narrated and recalled some childish pranks and even told a few jokes exposing his origins from the region of Campania.

I regret that, due to my own fault of not having sufficiently deepened knowledge of Padre with whom I had the privilege of earthly knowledge for many years, it was not sufficiently taken advantage of by me.

In the hopes of meeting again our beloved Padre in the near afterlife, due to advanced age, I thank you for the pleasure I felt in reading your wonderful book Padre Pio and I. I am pleased with you and this book and I cordially say goodbye.

L.L. from Foggia

Dear Mr. Affatato,

I am very grateful to you for the book Padre Pio and I, which you sent me after my request following the broadcast on "Porta a Porta," which I found literally fascinating by the fervor with which you spoke of Padre Pio.

After reading the book, I have completely changed my idea about this saintly Friar who had always been described to me as gruff and unfriendly. Now, however, through your moving testimony, I realize that you were close to a great saint. Your language penetrates the heart, and you cannot help but love Padre Pio.

Now I feel as if he is my own. It's as if he is close to me every day. And I owe this to you for letting me come to know him well in his true light.

I shall never tire of thanking God for this precious gift I received and that I will forever carry with me in my heart.

S.L. from Treviso

Adolfo, your book warms souls. Ever since I read it, I have begun praying to Padre Pio. Various circumstances had previously already led me to him, but until we met, I never unfortunately prayed to him.

My son M., now living in the Light, once exhorted me in a dream to "pray to the friar." And a good two years earlier, you and I, dear Adolfo, had the occasion of getting to know one other.

I am convinced that our meeting was led and strongly desired by Heaven. For all this and for the great love you give to your neighbor and especially to those greatly suffering, I thank you in my heart, Adolfo, together with my son and Padre. You are a beautiful soul.

See you soon.
M. P. C.

Dear Adolfo,

My name is N., I am 30 years old and I live in Piacenza with my husband, M., to whom I've been married for two years.

Let me begin by thanking you warmly for having recounted your experience with simplicity and warm light. It was invaluable for me.

I read your book in June during at a short vacation that M. and I took after a dark winter in which we were praying to an [image of the saint] which had given to us by some friends from San Giovanni Rotondo for our wedding.

I must clarify by saying that my husband and I were a little lukewarm in the faith at that time... Well, if I write to you now it's because your book "threw me out of the bed." It shook up my life incredibly and within a few months many things changed.

In the darkness in which my life was going, after reading your book, I prayed so much to be able to meet you and get in contact with you in the darkness I saw a distant light, but rationally it seemed very far away. I prayed, I prayed so much that if I only had your contact information, I would have asked you inasmuch as what you wrote in your book, inasmuch when Padre Pio said to you, "Only this..." Dear Adolfo, please intercede for me to Padre Pio and ask if I can become a spiritual daughter so that he can wait at the gates of eternal life also for me.

Dear Adolfo, since then so many things, as I said, have changed.

Padre Pio offered our prayers to the Blessed Mother and she called us on a long (and until then for us unthinkable) pilgrimage. In August, with Matthew we ended up in the car and went 5,000 km to Fatima Lourdes. I cannot tell her how many consolations we received on this trip and how many things unthinkable (for us) happened... How much light.

In mid-September we went down [to San Giovanni Rotondo] to say hello to Padre Pio and to thank him for his constant presence that we felt with us.

Now, we just returned from a cruise to celebrate our second wedding anniversary (January 6, 2008). This trip was another calling for us because it led us to the Holy Land.

Dear Adolfo, I do not know where our heavenly Mother will lead us next time. But, today I am now, thanks to Padre, more serene and happy, I humbly thank you so much for your great testimony.

I believe that my prayers back then arrived through you to Padre Pio ... I love him very much. Tell him the next time that "I feel him."

Thank you, thank you ... God bless you for this.

Sometimes (not often) I happen to come to Foggia to visit relatives, who knows if Padre Pio will have us meet. Meanwhile, an embrace, I will remember you in my prayers.

I love you,
N.

Dear Grandpa,

Each time we eat together, at the end of lunch, the stories of your life come out in which you were by the side of Padre Pio. I've always liked them and I was always fascinated, especially at the thought that you stood by the side of a Saint.

What I admire most of all is that after 42 years from his death, you continue to go to Mass by his tomb every Saturday.

Then, I always like to hear about the birth of my dad, and the miracle that Padre Pio did to have him be born, I cannot believe it.

After you wrote the book, Padre Pio and I, and the conferences you do throughout Italy purely out of charity for the poor, by now everyone knows you and I know how much you are appreciated.

Francesca and I are proud of you.

You're truly an authentic Grandpa!

I love you so much.

Your granddaughter,
Beatrice

Dearest Adolfo,

I read your book and enjoyed it. I cannot easily describe what I felt in learning about the knowledge and the journey you took in reaching the goal of spiritual son of St. Pio.

The way you expounded [the story] is clear and compelling, even surprising because it involves [your] real life, and deals with miracles which revealed themselves over time and involved, or I should say, changed your life.

I found it moving because it thoroughly affects the psyche of those who pursue the rosary of precious stones made by knowledge and devotion, and by casualness of relationship with Padre.

I thank you for allowing me to read your precious little book and I embrace you together with your loved ones.

With much affection
A.R. from Bari

Dear Mr. Affatato,

I received, through my husband, your beautiful book about your experiences alongside Padre Pio. I devoured it in two days. My hands are still trembling with emotion, and I shall not hide the fact that my face was streaked with tears several times, because as I read the book, I could see, as if it were live, everything you were describing.

Even now I see before me Padre who rests his crucified hand on my head to comfort me; yes, because Mr. Affatato, less than a year ago, I lost a son who was 18 years old. I then entered into a very serious form of depression. For me, life had no meaning; I lived each day in excruciating memory of my son. And all the love which my husband and our other children surrounded me seemed to be worth nothing.

Then, suddenly the heavens granted me a great gift: your book, Padre Pio and I.

I read it, once, then twice. And the more I went on, the more I noticed a serenity growing and taking possession of my body. A miracle was about to take place: thanks to the many episodes I read about the extraordinary nature of this Holy Friar, I regained confidence once again in life, I started to live in the sweet memory of my son, who is today a being of light, a new angel in heaven.

My gratitude for you will never end for being an instrument of God through Padre Pio, in bringing -- through his testimony -- great serenity in my life.

Always keep doing what you are doing. You do not know how much good you can do for people. Now I understand that the only way I can continue to have my son live in my earthly life is through continual prayer. Only with the daily rosary -- as the heavenly mother is always asking us -- can be a soothing balm that relieves pain while waiting to meet him once again in the divine light where there is no more suffering.

I beseech you that when you go to the tomb of Padre to remember my son in prayer.

A huge hug from a mother's pained heart, as I say to you again thank you ... thank you.

A.M. from Rome

Dear Mr. Affatato,

It was one of the most restless periods of my life. I am not sure what was making me [feel] so... It's true that I had problems at work, but I had had them for several years and did not understand why they were weighing so much on my mood. There were more in the months of June and July 2009, and shortly thereafter I realized what it was.

While at my new job, I was talking with a colleague who was very devout. She recommended I go to confession and get closer to God, because that would be the only way I would be able to get the peace I wanted. I thought about it and thought about it. Finally, I went into a church and the priest was not there; I went back, but I did not have the courage.

I am separated from my husband and I have a child with a man who is not my husband. Who knows? Maybe God did not want me! But instead, on Wednesday, August 12, around 10:30 am, I was able to confess in a river of tears and I asked the priest to offer a Mass in remembrance of my father and a person dear to me, who both died a long time ago, but for whom I asked to intercede, not knowing why, between me and God.

On August 14, my son was diagnosed with high risk ALL (Acute Lymphocytic Leukemia) and with only a 30% chance to live beyond the first two weeks. It's been over a year and G. and I are still together. God called me to him to confront this path together. I could not do it alone, I did not have enough strength.

On Saturday, August 16, I returned to church and asked the priest for a special blessing for me and G. While wearing liturgical vestments, he did so without thinking twice. I do not know if the blessed oil was scented, I don't think it was, but indeed I smelled a great fragrance of roses, and from then on neither God nor Padre Pio (and I say Father because for me it is the Father who protects us), nor Our Lady have ever abandoned us.

I pray every day, sometimes with anger, other times with fright, others with immense love. But it doesn't matter how I feel because they are there to listen to me and understand me and accept me. Now I am certain that there is a place for me in their presence. God called me, Mary dries up all my tears, and Padre Pio is close to me each moment of my day. And I became aware of this in reading your testimony of life lived with him.

His suffering was be a way to relieve ours. Never in life have I felt more loved and protected! Every day that passes is a gift to us, and I try in all ways to return all the love of those who are close to us, to my son, and to those who suffer. Perhaps I do not do so perfectly, but I am grateful in having received a second chance to live life illuminated by God.

I hope all this lasts a long time, and in the suffering that we live I will never stop feeling fortunate because my son is still with me and I embrace him with the love of all those mothers who no longer have their children to embrace.

I thank you, Adolfo, but before you, T., your sister, to whom Padre Pio has given immense power: to love one's neighbor and to care for them precisely in the moments and ways in which we are not able to do. You have given me the knowledge of this great man and I will do everything in my power to deserve him, with the prayer that every child in the world should have the opportunity to live in their own right as children.

The first trip that G. and I will make will be there to San Giovanni Rotondo. G. himself, without knowing anything, one evening in the living room while playing with my mother exclaimed, "Grandma, what perfume are you wearing? Roses?" And when I heard this, I cried with joy, because I know that Padre Pio will accompany him at every moment of his life, and even more so in those moments when I can no longer look after my most precious love and take care of him.

Thank you
L. and G.

In 1999, I experienced something dramatic in my life involving my wife involuntarily. It was an experience which was eventually resolved in the best way and it inevitably permitted me to rebuild my relationship with God that had been broken for a long time.

During that period, I prayed a lot and had a lot of hope. And without fanaticism or particular beliefs, I felt the need for a witness of faith, which I then found in the life, works, knowledge of and prayers of Padre Pio. In that period, he was a constant presence and a spiritual guide for me. I read everything about him, so great was the need to satiate myself with his holiness and to increase my knowledge of this saint who felt like part of the family. Since then, ten years of normality have passed. I'll never forget, however, in every moment that special relationship that was created between me and him to finalize that dramatic time.

Last year I happened to be in the law firm of a friend of mine when I saw a book on his desk. On the cover was a photo of Padre Pio and a young layman in the act of kissing his hand. I picked up the book and my friend, seeing my curiosity, said that he would provide a copy of it for me right away since the author was a good friend of his. My friend kept his promise and a few days later he gave me a copy of Padre Pio and I. My curiosity was strong and I read the book in one breath that same evening.

I was moved often while reading the words which were so sincere in relating events experienced first-hand by the author which were not the result of bibliographic or journalistic research. I clearly perceived the freshness of the direct contact, but I especially had the impression of getting to know Padre directly in his simplicity and I immediately felt like I was the protagonist -- as if I had personally lived part of my life with a saint as one of my own family members whom I had never known!

I do not know if it was due to Adolfo Affatato or a reflection of Padre Pio that transmitted through the author to others; I only know that something has changed within me. And now, perhaps because I always keep the book on my bedside table, I have the distinct feeling of knowing Padre well. He who continues to transmit to me, more than before, hope and strength in weakness, which for me is love.

V.T.B. from Francavilla al Mare

Epilogue

In the Foreword, we mentioned how we "randomly" met Adolfo and his wife Franca on a train going to Rome in 2013. When he asked if we could help get his book published in English, we did not know where to begin.

With the help of many people along the way, we were able to make this book a reality to share with the English speaking audience. Since our first meeting, we have had the opportunity to meet Adolfo on other trips to San Giovanni Rotondo and learn more about his relationship with Padre Pio.

Adolfo is very devoted to Padre Pio. He is hoping with his book now in English, that many people will get to know Padre Pio "more and better".

We are very grateful to him personally. As told in the Foreword, we were in very difficult family situation with our daughter. When we returned to San Giovanni Rotondo in 2014, he pulled out the picture of our daughter from his wallet and prayed with us at the tomb of Padre Pio. We had given him her picture the year before on the train when we told him out story.

He pulled out her picture again a year later when we met with Fr. Cuvino to discuss having the English version available at the friary. Fr. Cuvino prayed over the picture along with a glove of Padre Pio and a small crucifix Padre Pio kept at his bedside.

Within the next year we were reunited with our daughter and are thankful for the turnaround, and we visit her and our grandson on a regular basis in our home state of Missouri.

We are sure the intercessory prayers from Adolfo to Padre Pio, along with the prayers from family and friends, helped with our personal situation.

In this book Adolfo presents you, the reader, to Padre Pio. Adolfo once asked Padre Pio, "Father, will you promise me you will bless everyone I present to you?" Padre Pio's response was firm, "Yes, now and when I'm gone."

The pictures on the following pages share some of our experiences during this 2 1/2 year project. We hope to continually update those interested in Adolfo's journey as a spiritual son of Padre Pio through a website at www.PadrePioAndI.Org.

Steve and Lynne Pfaff
Clearwater, FL

Adolfo on the train to Rome in September of 2013.
He is holding first-class relics and a picture of Padre Pio.

Adolfo with passenger Luca de Masi. Luca boarded the train and became the translator into English for Adolfo's stories about Padre Pio.

Adolfo and Lynne Pfaff were good friends by the end of the train ride to Rome.

Adolfo and Franca with family and friends outside San Salvatore in Lauro church in Rome. Each year on September 22nd, a Mass is held at this church to celebrate the last full day of Padre Pio's life. This photo was taken in 2013.

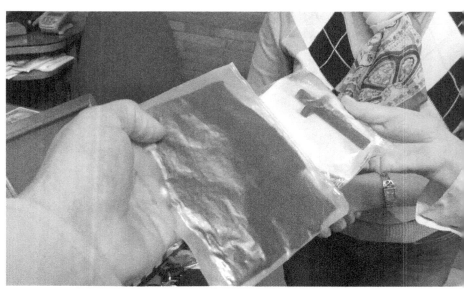

This a glove worn by Padre Pio to cover his stigmata, and a small crucifix he kept on the night stand next to his bed.

Our Lady of Grace Church. Padre Pio said Mass at this alter from his arrival in 1916 until the newer church was built next door in 1959.

The crucifix in the choir loft of the old church that Padre Pio was praying to when he received the stigmata in 1918. Padre Pio is the first priest in the history of the Church to receive the stigmata.

The newer church where Padre Pio said his last Mass in 1968.

Father Paolo Cuvino at the friary of Padre Pio in San Giovanni Rotondo.

Padre Pio crypt surrounded by mosaics designed
by world famous artist Fr. Marko Rupnik.

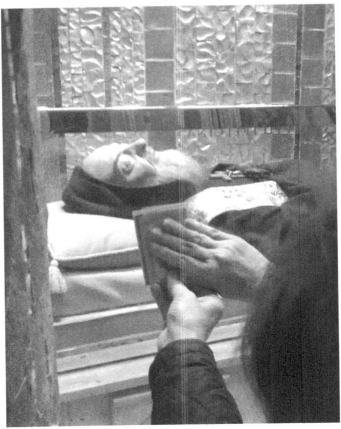

Adolfo and Franca with Steve and Lynne Pfaff after a tour of
the friary and shrine in San Giovanni Rotondo in 2014.

The Shrine of Padre Pio was dedicated in 2004.
The relics of his body are in the lower level of this building.

210

Contact Information

Adolfo Affatato

Adolfo, as a young man, was called by name out of a crowd by Padre Pio. He had never met Padre Pio prior to that day. Padre Pio said "I have been waiting many years for you". That day began the journey as a Spiritual Son of Padre Pio.

Adolfo shares his personal stories over the last 15 years of Padre Pio's life. The stories are inspiring, touching and personal. This first-time English edition includes the original Italian version and some all-new chapters added for this printing. Adolfo and his wife, Franca, reside in Foggia, Italy. Adolfo can be reached via email at: AdolfoAffatato@Libero.it

Bret Thoman

Bret Thoman, OFS has a master's degree in Italian from Middlebury College in Vermont, a BA in foreign languages from the University of Georgia, and a certificate in Franciscan studies from St. Francis University in Pennsylvania.

He has translated twelve books from Italian to English on spiritual and religious subjects. Bret also interpreted for CNN during the papal conclave and announced the election of Pope Francis live on the air. Additionally, he has his FAA pilot's license and has logged over 3,500 hours of flight time as a flight instructor and regional airline pilot. However, his main occupation is organizing pilgrimages for St. Francis Pilgrimages, the company he founded in 2004. He has been a member of the Secular Franciscan Order since 2006 when he made his lifelong profession. He currently lives in Loreto, Italy with his wife and their two children.

He can be reached at: *bret.thoman@gmail.com*.

Steve and Lynne Pfaff

Steve and Lynne Pfaff were on a personal holy pilgrimage in Italy in 2013 and on a train from San Giovanni Rotondo to Rome they met Adolfo Affatato and formed a friendship with him. Adolfo asked them to help get his book about Padre Pio into English.

That began a two-year project that led them to finding the right people to help them complete this English publication. They are business owners and reside in Clearwater, Florida.

They can be reached at:

Steve@PadrePioAndl.Org or Lynne@PadrePioAndl.Org

Made in the USA
Monee, IL
30 October 2022

16846887R00125